Advance Praise for
My China in Tang Poetry

"Susan Wan Dolling has lived with Tang poetry for decades, and like the best teachers she knows how to make her familiarity ours. She tells the stories behind the poems, and her translations, clear and natural and fluid, have a sure sense of how emotions build and shine. Far more than an anthology, this series is a comprehensive tour of Tang poetry and culture with a genial, expert and witty guide."
— James Richardson Poet, Professor of Creative Writing, Emeritus, Lewis Center for the Arts, Princeton University

"This book makes me want to drop everything and do nothing but learn about Chinese poetry! Dolling brings poets Li Bai and Du Fu vividly to life, both in her translations and in the stories she tells about 8th-century China, along with her own memories about growing up in Hong Kong. The notes to the poems cover poetics, wordplay, proverbs, history, geography, legends, folk songs, festivals, food, flowers, and more—everything you need to fall in love with these poems, these poets, and their world."
— Laura Gibbs, author of *Aesop's Fables: A New Translation*, Penguin Classics

"Susan Wan Dolling's fresh translations of Tang poetry is a virtuoso performance...with vivid context and engaging personal anecdotes, Dolling's work interprets the Tang dynasty and its literary luminaries for a new generation of readers."
— Kevin Peraino author of *A Force So Swift: Mao, Truman, and the Birth of Modern China, 1949*, Crown Publishing

"Susan Wan Dolling has given readers, from academics to lovers of poetry, a refreshing and innovative staging of Tang poetry. Informed personal readings accompanied by stories behind the poets and poems capture the enduring appeal of Tang poetry. In my many years of teaching Classical Chinese poetry, this series is a fresh take that is accessible to the general audience unfamiliar with Chinese as well as being delightful for the audience steeped in the tradition (and everyone in between)."
—Chiu-Mi Lai, Ph.D., Professor of Instruction, University of Texas at Austin

"Susan Wan Dolling's My China in Tang Poetry is surprisingly easy and entertaining reading. Susan's scholarship as well as vivid imagination shine through her storytelling and educated postulations, informative for both Tang poetry aficionados and neophytes. Her resplendent translations of the Chinese poetry are brilliant."
—Diana Lin, Hong Kong Journalist

"These volumes are a must for anyone who is interested in the Tang poetry which is the heart of the literature and culture of China."
—Margaret Sun, author of *Betwixt and Between,* Earnshaw Books

"Susan Wan Dolling is a scholar/poet who has breathed and danced these poems every day of her life. These beautiful translations are proof positive that translation is never a matter of just translating words. Thank you, Susan, for this gift of poetry."
—Nadia Benabid, translator of *Return to Painting* by Nobel Laureate Gao Xingjian

"In China, past and present, most kids grow up reciting Tang poems, and some even try their hand at writing these five or seven character lines when they feel inspired. Writing in the genre, usually poems of four or eight lines, might sound simple, but in fact it is not. As one grows older and read more and more of the annotated texts, one becomes more and more appreciative of the details of both the artistry and historical richness of these poems. As translator and annotator of these Tang poems, Susan Wan Dolling has done a fantastic job. The meticulousness of her annotations should be appreciated, and her renderings, accurate and smoothly readable (both script-wise and sound-wise) are definitely enjoyable."

—Diana Yue, Honorary Associate Professor, Hong Kong University, translator of *Flying Carpet: A Tale of Fertillia* by Hong Kong's own Xixi

"Best book ever!"

—Li Bai, poet and drunkard

唐詩

FRIENDS AND LOVERS

MY CHINA IN TANG POETRY
VOLUME III

温淑寧

Susan Wan Dolling

Friends And Lovers
My China in Tang Poetry Volume III

By Susan Wan Dolling

Trade Paper: 978-988-8904-07-5
Digital: 978-988-8904-05-1

© 2024 Susan Wan Dolling

Photographer: Clare Dyer

POETRY / TRANSLATION

EB226

All rights reserved. No part of this book may be reproduced in material form, by any means, whether graphic, electronic, mechanical or other, including photocopying or information storage, in whole or in part. May not be used to prepare other publications without written permission from the publisher except in the case of brief quotations embodied in critical articles or reviews. For information contact info@earnshawbooks.com

Published in Hong Kong by Earnshaw Books Ltd.

For my families in Hong Kong, China,
England, Canada, and the U.S.A.

Contents

Basic Information		1
Preamble		2
Chapter One	The Poetry of Two Exiles:	
	Liu Zongyuan and Liu Yuxi	11
Chapter Two	Abiding Love, Xiang Ling: Bai Juyi	36
Chapter Three	Bai Juyi's Love of Folk and Country	65
Chapter Four	Yuan-Bai Friendship	81
Chapter Five	Yuan Zhen and His Flowers	97
Chapter Six	A Ghostly Talent: Li He	104
Chapter Seven	Du Mu: A Sensual Man	147
Chapter Eight	The Mysterious Mr. Li Shangyin	170
Endnote: Verse Forms		193
Poets and Dates		196
Acknowledgements		197
Epilogue		200

Basic Information

Some background information may be useful for those unfamiliar with the Chinese language in English. The dominant system for Romanizing Chinese used to be the Wade-Giles system. Wade and Giles were two 19th Century British sinologists. After the communist victory in 1949, a new system of Romanization of the spoken word was created, called *Pinyin*, which simply means "phonetics" in Chinese. The government of the People's Republic under Mao Zedong also created a Modified form of the written Chinese language, known as "Simplified Chinese", largely to make Chinese characters easier to learn and therefore promote universal education. In feudal society, the written language belonged only to the privileged. For the sake of simplicity, I mainly use Pinyin in these books. Exceptions are noted. For Chinese characters, I use the traditional or standard script (繁體/正體) because a systematized simplified script (簡體) simply did not exist in Tang China!

    A quick word on names that come up so often in these stories. In feudal China, a person's birth name 名 *ming*, is used only by elders and the emperor. Friends and peers or someone in a younger generation calls one by one's courtesy name 字 *zi*. Then there is the pen name 別號 *bie hao*, which can be used to refer to oneself or used by others among the literati. To simplify matters, I simply call them by the name (or names) by which we know them best in literature.

Preamble

Friendships fostered among men are some of the most meaningful and profound relationships in Tang times. No one else besides another scholar-official can share the complex psychology of being a scholar-official, or wanting to be one, and women, not even the most brilliant and learned among them, have no place in that world. In *Friends and Lovers*, we will be meeting three pairs of such friends who lived in the mid-Tang period that came after the chaos that changed everything, the An Lushan Rebellion of 755-756. The first two pairs of friends were 柳宗元 Liu Zongyuan and 劉禹錫 Liu Yuxi, and 白居易 Bai Juyi and 元稹 Yuan Zhen. The third pair, Liu Yuxi and Bai Juyi, were to become close friends in later life, when Liu Zongyuan and Yuan Zhen had both died in their forties.

Liu Yuxi and Bai Juyi were born in the same year, 772, and Liu Zongyuan was only a year younger. Yuan Zhen was born the latest among them, in 779. As it happened, the two Lius (notice these are different characters) passed their exams at the same time and, several years later, Bai Juyi and Yuan Zhen also passed the Imperial Exam at the same time. These were politically fraught times. In their lifetimes (772-846), for example, there were eight emperors, from Daizong to Wuzong, two of whom were killed, and Shunzong, 順宗, the emperor in whose reign the short-lived Yongzhen Reforms 永貞革新 (805) took place, reigned only for one year. The Yongzhen Reforms were a failure, and since both Liu Zongyuan and Liu Yuxi were enthusiastic participants, this year saw their promising careers destroyed. After working together for almost a decade, they were then

MY CHINA IN TANG POETRY

demoted and sent away from the capital to the provinces in "the south". During this time, the south of China was not built up or prosperous as it is today. The south was where pesky ministers seen as troublemakers were banished. Thus, the two of them were sent, one to Yongzhou and one to Lianzhou. Many others, sympathetic to their cause, were also sent away. Though their political careers declined, however, their poetry benefitted from the gain in perspective of having to live very differently. Long story short, their political careers never got back on track. After about a decade away, they were recalled to the capital, but predictably, this was not to last long. After their short reunion in Chang'an, when Liu Yuxi was banished again, this time, to the even more remote Bozhou, because of a satirical poem he wrote, Liu Zongyuan petitioned the court to let him take his friend's place in consideration of Liu Yuxi's eighty-year-old mother who would have to go with him. He was unsuccessful but, eventually with the help of friends, able to change Liu Yuxi's post to the less remote province of Lianzhou. This time, Liu Zongyuan himself was banished to Liuzhou. Liu Zongyuan was to die in Liuzhou in Guangxi, at age forty-seven. He left all his work and his children to Liu Yuxi's care.

The following poem by Liu Zongyuan was written after their short reprieve in Chang'an. When they had to leave the capital, they were able to travel partway together. Posterity has found the following poem very moving, as it showed us both the deep feelings Liu Zongyuan had for his friend as well as how it foreshadowed one of those jokes life often plays on us, whereby his dearest friend was to spend old age with another poet, Bai Juyi, in the way he had hoped to do. Bai Juyi and Liu Yuxi were to live next door to each other for six years near the end of their lives. In this poem, as in numerous others. these poets wrote back and forth to each other, they called each other by their courtesy names; Liu's was Mengde 夢得. Mengde means "received in a dream," just as his birth name, 禹錫 Yuxi, means "gift from Yu," as his mother said that she dreamt the mythological King Yu came to her in a dream with the infant in his arms when she was pregnant with him. "Heaven" on line 3, refers to the Emperor.

PARTING AGAIN FROM MENGDE

For twenty years we shared good times and bad.
Today we have reached another fork in the road.
If Heaven allows us to return home to our farms,
I'd be your neighbor: share our days as old men.

重別夢得

二十年來萬事同，
今朝岐路忽西東。
皇恩若許歸田去，
晚歲當爲鄰舍翁。

In this volume we will begin with these two friends, before moving onto what I call Bai Juyi's three loves, one of whom was Yuan Zhen.

In high school, I had thought that "Curse of Passion," better known as the "Song of Everlasting Sorrow", was about Xuanzong and his Imperial Consort, and even when I first translated it in college, that it was a historical narrative. I was not wrong, except that I was to find out, when I reacquainted myself with Bai Juyi, that it was quite a bit more personal than that. This second story will be told in the following chapter on his "Abiding Love".

MY CHINA IN TANG POETRY

Personally, however, the Bai Juyi poem that made the greatest imprint on my life was the shorter, and some might say, simpler "Swallow Song" and after that his "Pipa Song". Let me explain. "Swallow Song" was another one of those poems I was "made" to memorize. It was in the summer between Second and Third grades (or Primary Two and Three as we called them in Hong Kong) that my mother set it as the first lesson I had to learn. My mother was not a "Tiger Mom," as we've learned to call Chinese mothers who are ambitious for their children to get on in the world and drive them to excel. In fact, making me recite a few poems every summer in elementary school was about all the "discipline" she could enforce on me. I can't even remember why I was amenable to the exercise, as I was not exactly an obedient child. Maybe bribery was involved, or, more likely than not, I just wanted to please her. Now I wonder whether, in fact, I liked the feel of the words in my mouth, and that was the reason why I complied.

"Swallow Song" is almost like a child's nursery rhyme, harmless, on first encounter, but like some English nursery rhymes and fairytales, one notices a dark side to them as one learns to decipher them. "Swallow Song" sounded like a ditty, a simple song about a mother bird and her four babies, just like my mother, who had four children, my two brothers, my sister and me. There was a father bird in it, too, but the heavy lifting of child-rearing seemed to have been done by the mother bird, just as with our parents, so it seemed to my childish eyes. If I chirped it as a bird song, however, I discovered in my teenage years that my mother had chosen it for the hidden message of gratitude in it, gratitude for one's parents, or so she told me. I did not like to be coerced into anything, and even though I had no reason not to be grateful to my parents, I loathed the overt manipulation. Many years later, when I started to translate poetry though, the poem snuck back into my waking mind, and I discovered yet again that I had only half-understood the poem. Eventually, it took me another three decades to mould the translation to my satisfaction, and while doing the research, I discovered the poet's introduction to the poem, which turned the message upside down. This will be explained when we get to the poem.

My relationship with the "Pipa Song" is somewhat less complex. I must have had it in a Chinese literature class in secondary school. Again, it remained dormant until I started translating, and then it appealed to me particularly as a poem *about* translation. The sympathetic relationship between the poet and the pipa player felt to me very much like my relationship with the poets I chose to translate. Our lives were very different, but in one way or another, the sentiments evoked by their poetry spoke of my own experience, or at least moved in me something I could relate to, sometimes quite unexpectedly.

In spending a prolonged period with Bai this time, I found more buried treasures in his poetry than I could have imagined from my previous, limited acquaintance with him. The Bai Juyi I had previously known was an old man. Perhaps he felt especially old to me as a young person, because everything he had to say seemed to come with some lesson or other. It was as if my mother's Confucius came with him. This time around, I started with the little boy, and watched him fall in love and then, be thwarted, not by the girl he loved, but by his mother who would not give her permission to their marriage. This knowledge helped me see the beginnings of his most famous poems in the early ones written during this time of frustration.

Liu Zongyuan, Liu Yuxi, Bai Juyi and Yuan Zhen are, chronologically, considered mid-Tang poets. After them came

MY CHINA IN TANG POETRY

the so-called Late Tang poets, a decadent lot. I have chosen three of them for this brief introduction to their poetry. Li He is, chronologically, a mid-Tang poet, but his ghostly poems have persuaded most scholars to call him "late". I shall let Li He's idiosyncrasies speak for themselves when we come to his poetry.

Du Mu and Li Shangyin are called the Minor Li/Du (not Du/Li, even though Du Mu is older than Li Shangyin) because of the Major Li/Du, Li Bai and Du Fu, who came almost exactly a hundred years before them. The fact that they are even allowed to sing in the minor key after those giants shows their importance in the Chinese literary tradition. In other words, just as Li Bai and Du Fu are held up as the best in High Tang poetry, Du Mu and Li Shangyin are recognized as the best among the Late Tang poets. The two apparently met once when Li Shangyin was still a young man. Eleven years Du Mu's junior. Coincidentally, their age difference was just like that between Du Fu and Li Bai and, Li Shangyin was an admirer of the already established older poet, Du Mu. The two apparently had a good conversation, but this did not develop into those life-long friendships between two empathetic souls like that of the major Li/Du. One political incident, though, did affect these men's lives significantly, even though neither of them were directly involved, unlike the Yongzhen Reforms that wrecked Liu Zongyuan and Liu Yuxi's careers. This was the so-called Sweet Dew Incident 甘露事變 that took place on December 14, 835, under the reign of Emperor Wenzong 文宗.

In 835, Du Mu was age thirty-two and Li Shangyin was twenty-three. As mentioned before, by this time, the Tang emperors were ruling in name only. It was the eunuchs who had the real power. These "non-men", as they were sometimes called, had been gradually gaining political power in every sphere of government over the last century since the time of Gao Lishi, the eunuch Li

Bai offended. Between these two pairs of poets' lifetimes, the six or seven emperors were all controlled by eunuchs in one way or another.

Du Mu came from a prominent family and was in mid-career by the time the Sweet Dew Incident happened and might be counted fortunate, as the resulting reshuffle only meant he was sent away from the capital, which was his home, and given minor responsibilities in the provinces, though not as far away as the other poets we have seen. Li Shangyin, who came from a poor family, as we shall see in the chapter devoted to his poetry, was more affected by the contentious fighting between two factions, the Li clan versus the Niu clan, because his mentor was a member of the Niu clan, and his in-laws belonged to the Li clan.

The Sweet Dew Incident was a palace coup, involving the emperor and the eunuchs. Emperor Wenzong, supported by his two closest allies, Chancellor Li Xun and General Zheng Zhu. Together, they hatched a plan to lure all the powerful eunuchs to one place to observe what was believed to be an auspicious omen for the emperor, that is, dew frozen on branches of the pomegranate tree. Invitations were sent out to the eunuchs announcing that this phenomenon had been observed and summoned them to come to one of the palaces where imperial soldiers loyal to the emperor would be lying in wait. However, the eunuchs had spies everywhere, and one of them smelled a rat, investigated, and laid a trap for the emperor's men. Instead of killing off the eunuchs, Wenzong's allies and about a thousand others were slaughtered. The eunuchs spared Wenzong, but he was thereafter under their collective thumb.

This historical shroud may partly explain the shadows in the poetry of Minor Li/Du. In any case, it has persuaded commentators, especially those who want to see more patriotic fervour in their poets, to suggest there are more allusions to political intrigue and/or ambition in their poetry than meets the eye. I shall leave those interpretations to them. What I shall present to you are the two poets as I know them, one a sensual man like the King of Han in Bai's "Curse of Passion". His enjoyment of such beauties, however, as centuries of critics have agreed, is one of "pure pleasure unsullied by lust" 樂而不淫. Even though Du Mu's poetry is not without sadness and regret, compared to that of the mysterious, and I imagine him as elegant, Li Shangyin, Du Mu seems to be the less troubled and complex of the two. Li Shangyin has attracted much attention, especially in recent years, from scholars and translators, perhaps because of the mysteries and complexities of his writings. Much research has been done and more will no doubt be forthcoming.

1

Liu Zongyuan 柳宗元 and Liu Yuxi 劉禹錫
The Poetry of Two Exiles

Do opposites really attract? Looking at the poetry of the pairs of lifelong friends in this series—Li Bai and Du Fu, Bai Juyi and Yuan Zhen, Liu Zongyuan and Liu Yuxi, although not so much Wang Wei and Pei Di—we have to agree. What Liu Zongyuan and Liu Yuxi shared, beyond mutual admiration, was their almost identical life experiences and how they adapted to their fates after their banishment to the south. Let us begin with Liu Zongyuan.

Born into a prominent family, his political and literary talents were recognized early on in life, but in 805, in his thirty-second year, because of his part in the failed Yongzhen Reforms, he was demoted and exiled to Yongzhou, Hunan, and later, to Liuzhou, Guangxi, far from the capital. He died, at age forty-six in Guangxi where there is now a statue and memorial park built for him. Liu Zongyuan is honored by posterity as one of the Eight Prose Masters of the Tang and Song Period, but his poetry must be included in our appreciation of his life's work. The following are five of his best-known poems. They also happen to delineate his changing perspective.

Bayberries is a southern fruit. To name them is to tell us where he was, in the south, where he was sent. A rainy period comes with its ripening and is called bayberry rain. If you've never tried this fruit, you should, it is tasty and unusual.

We see gibbons often in Chinese poetry, and their call is so piercing that it would make quite an impression on anyone hearing them for the first time. Scientists sometimes call them "lesser apes". They can grow to three feet tall, and they move swinging by their long arms from tree to tree. They are found in southern China, India, and Borneo. Their fur can be brown, black, or blonde and they have monkey-like faces. And they are noisy creatures, "singing" and "howling" all day long. Sometimes, in the mornings, they even sing in duets. And some, mate for life. Chinese people find their call extremely sad. Thus, the expression that if you hear "the gibbons cry three times, tears are bound to fall." This sentiment is from a fisherman's song and this line is found in Du Fu's "Autumn Songs", near the end of *Superstars*.

Besides gibbons, another phenomenon often found in these classical poems, is the fact that rivers in China tend to flow eastward to the sea because of China's topography. In the next poem, however, Liu's river is said to "flow relentlessly north". Perhaps Liu is talking about a small inland river. More likely, it is the river in his mind that is flowing north, back to the capital. Liu calls what I have translated as "clouds" on the river "snow", but it seems to me unlikely that snow is still floating on the river by this time of year, so that white clumps he sees floating on the river are probably clouds that he's calling snow; you are welcome to put the snow back in the river if you so wish. Then, there is the image of one's "[pure] white robe" being dyed "black" (last line) by dust, which has been used by such poets as Xie Tiao 謝朓 and Lu Ji 陸機, to connote stain, as in corruption. In this poem, Liu turns the idea upside down, and this inky stain is seen as something desirable, because using ink means working, and working means serving the country, and at this point, Liu

MY CHINA IN TANG POETRY

was still stuck in the mentality that this can only be done at the capital, the seat of power. Now, we are ready for the first poem.

BAYBERRY RAIN

Bayberries ripen in time to greet the season's endless rain,
like a blackout curtain drawn over these last spring days.
In the south, nights are consumed by the gibbon's grief,
and dawn comes with loud cockcrows, shattering dreams.
Fog on the sea reaches all the way to its southernmost tip.
Clouds on the river roll relentlessly to the unreachable north.
My clean, white robe is soaked through with this inky drizzle,
though this ink is nothing like the dust at the nation's capital.

梅雨

梅實迎時雨，
蒼茫值晚春。
愁深楚猿夜，
夢斷越雞晨。
海霧連南極，
江雪暗北津。
素衣今盡化，
非為帝京塵。

ON HEARING THE GIBBON'S CALL AT YELLOW CREEK

A winding path along Yellow Creek goes on and on.
The gibbons along the creek wail just as relentlessly,
but this banished minister has no more tears to shed.
Pointless, their heartbreaking performance for me.

FRIENDS AND LOVERS

入黃溪聞猿

溪路千里曲，
哀猿何處鳴。
孤臣淚已盡，
虛作斷腸聲。

PASSING BY A DESERTED VILLAGE IN SOUTH VALLEY ONE AUTUMN MORNING

Late autumn one morning, I passed by a lonesome valley.
Frost had descended and branches hung heavy in frozen dew.
A little bridge over the brook was covered with yellow leaves.
A deserted village had become a wild patch of old woodland.
Unassuming flowers, braving the cold, held on here and there,
and spring water was still making intermittent tinkling noises.
Have I not left my scheming heart behind a long time ago,
why then are deer still afraid and run away when I appear?

秋曉行南谷經荒村

杪秋霜露重，
晨起行幽谷。
黃葉覆溪橋，
荒村唯古木。
寒花疏寂歷，
幽泉微斷續。
機心久已忘，
何事驚麋鹿？

MY CHINA IN TANG POETRY

THE FISHERMAN

At nightfall, the fisherman sought shelter by the Western Rock.
Up with dawn, he cooks a simple meal with the water of Xiang.
By the time the sun comes out, he's gone with the morning mist,
headed into the clear green waves with a long sigh of his oar.
He gazes upstream on the horizon where the river disappears.
His heart is with the clouds chasing each other around the hills.

漁翁

漁翁夜傍西巖宿，
曉汲清湘燃楚竹。
煙銷日出不見人，
欸乃一聲山水綠。
回看天際下中流，
巖上無心雲相逐。

This next poem from Liu Zongyuan has inspired so many Chinese paintings that tourists to China would often come across them with the poem in calligraphy on such scrolls for sale. I offer you two renditions here:

RIVER SNOW (two translations)

Birds have all flown into the endlessly rolling hills.
Not a soul is seen along the empty mountain paths.
A lone boat, an old fisherman under a straw cape,
all by himself, fishing snow on half-frozen waves.

FRIENDS AND LOVERS

A thousand peaks, all birds gone,
numerous paths, no sign of anyone,
just an old fisherman in a straw cape
fishing: a lone boat on a river of snow.

江雪

千山鳥飛絕，
萬徑人蹤滅。
孤舟蓑笠翁，
獨釣寒江雪。

Notice how, with each successive poem, his complaint against his unfair lot becomes less and less noticeable until at last, peace descends, if not on him, at least on the scene that meets his eyes. His friend, Liu Yuxi met his fate less quietly. To his credit, he turned his indignation to appreciation of the very different, and in his eyes, far less sophisticated culture he was thrown into. Here is a song sequence he wrote in 822. I shall let him explain how it came about in his own Preface to the poems.

NINE SONGS OF BAMBOO BRANCHES (WITH PREFACE)
Songs from different places may be sung in different languages, but their music can be enjoyed by everyone. In my first New Year at Jianping, I heard some children singing "Song of Bamboo Branches" in the alley, accompanied by one playing the short flute, and one beating out a rhythm on a drum. The singers were dancing, lifting their sleeves like wings, and the one who sang the most was the champion. Their songs reminded me of the rich cadence of those found in the Huang Zhong Gong melodies, each ending with the full-throated finale of the folksongs of Wu. Even though I was not able to make out what they were saying,

MY CHINA IN TANG POETRY

yet the feelings they conveyed moved me as much as those of the Qi Yu from the *Book of Songs*. And like the poems Qu Yuan wrote when he was exiled to the watery regions of the Yuan and the Xiang. In them, he transformed the crude spirit songs of the primitive tribes and made them into his magnificent *Nine Songs*. The natives of Jingchu are still singing, dancing, and drumming to his *Nine Songs* in their religious rituals to this day. With that in mind, I composed the following nine verses to the tune of "Song of the Bamboo Branches" so that in the future others can trace them back to the folksongs of Ba where they originated.

1

Spring grass sprouting on the hills of White King City.
Clear water of the Shu flows beneath White Salt Peak.
Southern folks come to these hills to sing their songs,
northerners had better not be moved to think of home.

2

Peaks covered in wild peaches like heads full of flowers,
spring waters beat out the rhythm of Shu's rocky slopes.
Let not your love be like the crimson blooms that wither,
or my sadness will be as the river's endless rush to the sea.

3

Pretty pavilions on the rocky slopes, newly washed in rain,
like silk crinkles, ripples appear on the surface of Xiangxi.
Bridge east, bridge west, billowy willows adorn the shores,
to and fro, people come and go, singing as they stroll along.

FRIENDS AND LOVERS

4

The sun is three-bamboos-high in the sky, spring mist cleared.[1]
By the riverbanks, travellers' boats lined up one after another.
Will someone please take this letter to that wild man of mine,
he lives in Chengdu right alongside the thousand-mile-bridge.

5

Like a thick carpet of snow on the banks, wildflowers bloom.
Every household is celebrating, silver cups full of spring wine.
At Zhaojun Village, groups of women friends gather happily,
come from a spring outing on the outskirts of Yong'an Fort.[2]

6

West City Gate faces that hazardous boulder, Yan Yu Rock.
Year after year waves smash at it, but they can't make a dent.
Men's hearts are not resolute and strong as this piece of stone:
going east in their youth, coming back west, only to go again.

---

1   "Three-bamboos-high" means almost noon, sun's ascent measured by stalks of bamboos. Chengdu is the provincial capital and even in Tang times it was a glittery city.
2   Yong'an Fort is where Liu Bei, one of the "kings" of the Three Kingdom, set up court in White King City, and built this "palace" here after his lost a battle in 222. This is also where he was buried. Wang Zhaojun, one of the Four Great Beauties of China—her story is told in *Superstars*—was also from a village in these parts.

MY CHINA IN TANG POETRY

7

The twelve shoals of Bird Snare[3] are loud, crashing, clanging,
these waters have been dangerous passage since ancient times.
Regretfully men's hearts are not as passionate as this river,
bursting out of level ground, making irrepressible currents.

8

It's rainy season at Witch Mountain Gorges, mists rise like steam.
Voices of gibbons, clear and strong, call out from the highest trees,
travellers passing through will doubtless break down in tears:
it's not the gibbons' hearts breaking that make their calls so sad.

9

Tiers of peach blossoms upon tiers of pear on these hilly slopes,
From out of cloud-clad mountains, smoke rises from houses.
Women wearing gold and silver in their hair come to fetch water,
Men in straw hats, carrying machetes, prepare for spring farming.

---

3   Bird's Snare is my translation of Qutang, one of the Three Gorges, because *qu* 瞿 is an ancient character for the look of a bird's frightened eyes, too good an image to not bring across.

FRIENDS AND LOVERS

竹枝詞九首（並引）四方之歌，異音而同樂。歲正月，余來建平，裏中兒聯歌《竹枝》，吹短笛，擊鼓以赴節。歌者揚袂睢舞，以曲多為賢。聆其音，中黃鐘之羽，其卒章激訐如吳聲，雖傖儜不可分，而含思宛轉，有《淇奧》之豔。昔屈原居沅湘間，其民迎神，詞多鄙陋，乃為作《九歌》，到於今荊楚鼓舞之。故余亦作《竹枝詞》九篇，俾善歌者颺之，附於末，後之聆巴歈，知變風之自焉。

其一

白帝城頭春草生，
白鹽山下蜀江清。
南人上來歌一曲，
北人莫上動鄉情。

其二

山桃紅花滿上頭，
蜀江春水拍山流。
花紅易衰似郎意，
水流無限似儂愁。

其三

江上朱樓新雨晴，
瀼西春水縠文生。
橋東橋西好楊柳，
人來人去唱歌行。

其四

日出三竿春霧消，
江頭蜀客駐蘭橈。
憑寄狂夫書一紙，
家住成都萬里橋。

其五

兩岸山花似雪開，
家家春酒滿銀盃。
昭君坊中多女伴，
永安宮外踏青來。

其六

城西門前灩澦堆，
年年波浪不能摧。
懊惱人心不如石，
少時東去復西來。

其七

瞿塘嘈嘈十二灘，
此中道路古來難。
長恨人心不如水，
等閒平地起波瀾。

FRIENDS AND LOVERS

其八

巫峽蒼蒼煙雨時，
清猿啼在最高枝。
個裏愁人腸自斷，
由來不是此聲悲。

其九

山上層層桃李花，
雲間煙火是人家。
銀釧金釵來負水，
長刀短笠去燒畬。

Later, he wrote two more to the same folk tune, but instead of adding to the sequence of the nine, decided to present them as a separate pair of poems, perhaps wanting to keep the number nine to hark back to Qu Yuan's famous "Nine Songs".

TWO MORE SONGS OF BAMBOO BRANCHES
1

Green willows look greener still on calm lake water.
My love sings to me from somewhere across the lake.
The sun comes out in the east and rain falls on the west.
Is it a clear day or is it not, is your love like sun or rain?

MY CHINA IN TANG POETRY

2

Rain comes often to the Ba mountains and Chu waters.
The folk of Ba love to sing their native songs outdoors.
This morning I was longing for my home in the north,
by evening I am tapping to the music of the local songs.

竹枝詞二首
其一

楊柳青青江水平，
聞郎江上唱歌聲。
東邊日出西邊雨，
道是無晴卻有晴。

其二

楚水巴山江雨多，
巴人能唱本鄉歌。
今朝北客思歸去，
回入紇那披綠羅。

Next is a *jueju* with an unusual opening. It was probably written when he was still in the south. In this translation I had to move "this morning" from the third line to the second, and the "courtyard" from the third to the first. There is also the question of whether the wild geese are coming or going, because Liu used the word "sending [off]" in the second line about the wild geese. Normally, if he were in the north, the wild geese would be leaving in autumn, but since he was in the south, as he calls himself a "traveller" or "visitor" in the poem, the geese are arriving with the autumn. I am concluding that he was in the south.

FRIENDS AND LOVERS

BROUGHT ON BY THE AUTUMN WIND

A sudden gust blew autumn into my courtyard:
this morning, flocks of wild geese came flying by,
breaking the silence in the sky above the treetops.
The lonely visitor is always the first to hear them.

秋風引

何處秋風至？
蕭蕭送雁羣。
朝來入庭樹，
孤客最先聞。

This next piece was written between 824 and 826 when he was demoted a second time. This time, to Hezhou. The provincial governor there looked down on him, and made him move three times, each time to a smaller place until in the end he was moved to a tiny house the size of a room. Thus, he wrote this piece which might be called a prose poem or simply an inscription. The first four lines have become rather well-known. They are often used by those who feel slighted. At the end of the poem, he cites two important figures and their "shabby abodes" to make his final argument. Zhuge Liang is the famous strategist in the Three Kingdoms period. Yang Xiong was another famous statesman who petitioned his emperor and wrote a famous "reprimand" to which Liu Yuxi is alluding here. Both locations are situated at Shu, where he was exiled.

MY CHINA IN TANG POETRY

INSCRIPTION FOR MY SHABBY ABODE

A mountain is special not for its height,
but for the presence of an immortal in it.
A river is magical not for its depth, but
whether a dragon chooses to live there.
Though some call mine a shabby abode,
my conduct permeates it with the scent of virtue.
Green moss, like a thick carpet, grows up my steps.
Spring's sweetness wafts in my curtains.
Our lofty conversations are punctuated with laughter.
None who passes through here is stupid or ignorant.
We may strum simple tunes on my modest qin or share
a few passages from our treasured texts;
no cacophonous music to distract us,
no official documents or opinions to worry about.
Nanyang was graced by Zhuge's makeshift hut,
Yang Xiong's reprimand came from a Chengdu kiosk.
As Confucius said, "What are you calling shabby here?"

FRIENDS AND LOVERS

陋室銘
山不在高，
有仙則名。
水不在深，
有龍則靈。
斯是陋室，
惟吾德馨。
苔痕上階綠，
草色入簾青。
談笑有鴻儒，
往來無白丁。
可以調素琴，
閱金經。
無絲竹之亂耳，
無案牘之勞形。
南陽諸葛廬，
西蜀子雲亭。
孔子云：何陋之有？

In 826, Liu Yuxi and Bai Juyi met for the first time. They were both fifty-four years old, considered elderly in Tang times. Bai Juyi acknowledged Liu's contributions as a poet and bemoaned Liu's banishment from the capital for the last twenty-three years. The two exchanged poems and compliments and so their friendship began.

The next group of five poems were written by Liu at this time. Once again, Liu Yuxi gives us a preface that tells the story of their composition.

MY CHINA IN TANG POETRY

FIVE POEMS WRITTEN AT JINLING (WITH PREFACE)

When I was a young man, I had travelled to these parts, South of the River, but I have not toured Moling. Then, when I was sent to Liyang as prefect, I could only see it on tiptoe from far away. At the time, a visitor came by and showed me his "Five Poems Written at Jinling," which inspired me to write my own, and that is the origin of this set of poems. Later, I showed them to my friend, Bai Letian [that is, Bai Juyi], who chanted them appreciatively many times and proclaimed, "Poets who will come after us will not be able to surpass the lines in "Stone City" — "Waves knock hard on its empty door, roll back/ unanswered. Even though the other four poems are not as chantable as that, I dare say, nevertheless, they have not let Letian down.

STONE CITY

Ringed by mountains, Stone City ruins remain.
Waves knock hard on its empty door, rolls back
unanswered. East of Wei, the ancient moon shines on.
Night creeps across the ramparts much as it did before.

BLACK COAT ALLEY

Red Bird Bridge is overgrown with wild grass and wildflowers.
The sun sets into Black Coat Alley, sneaking in between houses.
Swallows used to build their nests in the eaves of royal palaces.
Now they fly into ordinary folks' porches, looking for shelter.

FRIENDS AND LOVERS

TERRACE CITY

Six Dynasties' kings and princes competing in displays of opulence,
and the most extravagant of all, Prince Chen's Spring Viewing Terrace,
but for his song of "Flowers in the Backyard," none would remember
the great halls and palaces buried under this piece of wild grass now.

MASTER SHENG'S LECTURE HALL

When Master Sheng takes the podium, even ghosts and spirits listen.[4]
Now that he has left us, there is no need to lock up even at night.
A layer of dust covers everything from top to bottom, nothing but
the brilliant light of the moon enters these hallowed halls anymore.

---

[4] Master Sheng was a monk who lived in the Jin Dynasty. Apparently he was such an inspired speaker of the scriptures that even stones nodded in agreement when he preached.

MY CHINA IN TANG POETRY

CHIEF MINISTER JIANG'S RESIDENCE

Southern Dynasty's Rhetorical Minister became Northern Dynasty's "guest."[5]
When he was allowed to return south, the Wei River was as clear as before.
Those seven odd acres of land by the bamboo grove at the terrace pond,
people these days say was where the Chief Minister once called home.

金陵五題 (並序)

余少為江南客，而未遊秣陵，嘗有遺恨。後為歷陽守，跂而望之。適有客以《金陵五題》相示，逌爾生思，欻然有得。他日友人白樂天掉頭苦吟，歎賞良久，且曰《石頭》詩云"潮打空城寂寞回"，吾知後之詩人，不復措詞矣。餘四詠雖不及此，亦不孤樂天之言耳。

石頭城

山圍故國周遭在，
潮打空城寂寞回。
淮水東邊舊時月，
夜深還過女牆來。

---

[5] This was the Prime Minister of the Southern Jin's Chen Dynasty, Jiang Zong (519-594). He was stranded in the north when the capital of Chen, Jiangling, fell.

FRIENDS AND LOVERS

烏衣巷

朱雀橋邊野草花，
烏衣巷口夕陽斜。
舊時王謝堂前燕，
飛入尋常百姓家。

台城

台城六代競豪華，
結綺臨春事最奢。
萬戶千門成野草，
只緣一曲後庭花。

生公講堂

生公說法鬼神聽，
身後空堂夜不扃。
高坐寂寥塵漠漠，
　一方明月可中庭

江令宅

南朝詞臣北朝客，
歸來唯見秦淮碧。
池台竹樹三畝餘，
至今人道江家宅。

As their friendship developed, the two poets exchanged many poems. The next poem was written as complement to Bai Juyi's "A Spring Tune" (829), a rather conventional "boudoir poem". What enlivens Bai's poem is the parrot, and, as we shall see in the next chapter, "Abiding Love", parrots are of particular interest to Bai Juyi, but first, here is "A Spring Tune":

A SPRING TUNE

She stays in her boudoir behind shadows of the flowering trees, with spring's melancholy sitting heavy on her delicate brows. Leaning against the balustrade, she turns her back to the parrot, deep in thought. What did she not want the bird to see and tell?

春詞

低花樹映小妝樓，
春入眉心兩點愁。
斜倚欄干臂鸚鵡，
思量何事不回頭？

Here is Liu Yuxi's complementary poem. Letian is Bai Juyi's courtesy name.

COMPANION POEM TO LETIAN'S SPRING TUNE

Newly made up, she came downstairs, ready to greet the day, to find spring locked in a garden full of misery and loveliness. Walking into its abundance, she idly counts the flowering buds, while a dragonfly chooses to land on the jade comb in her hair.

FRIENDS AND LOVERS

和樂天春詞

新妝宜面下朱樓，
深鎖春光一院愁。
行到中庭數花朵，
蜻蜓飛上玉搔頭。

This poem illustrates Liu Yuxi's outgoing and unconventional personality well. One wonders if he was moved to respond by the parrot, the most unconventional aspect of Bai's poem. His own poem is even more unconventional compared to other such "boudoir poems" which are usually written about young women stuck in their confined habitats, not allowed to "take more than three steps away from their bed chambers" if they were respectable ladies, according to Confucius. Often, classical poets have taken on their voices to speak of their own regrets. In Liu's poem, the young lady ventures out into the garden, and even out there feels "locked in". Her visitor, the dragonfly, is freer than she, and could "choose". Of course, this is my reading, the word "choose" is not explicit in the original; the dragonfly simply lands on her head.

In his last years, Liu had better luck with the authorities, and was made a prince's tutor, in Luoyang. As it happened, Bai Juyi was also tutor to one of the princes, not the same one, but also in Luoyang. For the last six years of his life, Liu Yuxi was able to be his friend's neighbour, as he built a house next to Bai. Between 837 and 838, the two wrote two sets of poems both titled "In Remembrance of Jiangnan". This is just one of many such "songs in response" 唱和, that the two wrote together. Jiangnan means "south of the river", the river being Chang Jiang, the Yangtze, or, as I have often called it, the Great River, the longest river in China. South of the river is the region of the Yangtze near its estuary. There are many poems by this title.

First, Bai Juyi's three poems. He had lived in these parts on three different occasions. In the second poem we find a mountain temple, this is Tianzhu Temple in Hangzhou. Cinnamon is the bark of cassias, and Qiantang is Qiantang Lake. In the third poem, we find Xishi again. She is said to look even more beautiful when tipsy. Yang Guifei, though she is not in this poem, has often been called a flower, like these Wu maids, and she too, is reputed to have been a beautiful drunk!

REMEMBERING JIANGNAN (THREE POEMS)

Jiangnan so beautiful,
I know well your splendid views:
day breaks like a wild flame spreading on your lively waves.
Your waters are bluer than the bluest grass in the springtime.
How can anyone not miss you?

In all of Jiangnan,
Hangzhou is the place I miss the most:
in the moonlight on that mountain temple, hunting for cassias,
lounging at the kiosk, watching Qiantang's tide roll out to sea.
Those were the days. Will they come again?

In all of Jiangnan,
that Wu Palace built for Xishi I also miss:
with a cup of Wu's finest wine, they call Tender Spring Bamboo,
watching pairs of Wu maids dance like drunken hibiscus in
 bloom.
Sooner or later, I must return for a visit!

FRIENDS AND LOVERS

憶江南詞三首

江南好，
風景舊曾諳。
日出江花紅勝火，
春來江水綠如藍。
能不憶江南？

江南憶，
最憶是杭州。
山寺月中尋桂子，
郡亭枕上看潮頭。
何日更重遊！

江南憶，
其次憶吳宮。
吳酒一杯春竹葉，
吳娃雙舞醉芙蓉。
早晚復相逢！

Now for Liu Yuxi's two poems:

REMEMBERING JIANGNAN

Spring is about to leave,
bowing in thanks to the man of Luoyang city.
Like slender willows in the breeze, she lifts her sleeves to wave goodbye.
Dew-soaked clusters of orchids as if wet with tears are just like maidens
sitting alone with brows tightly knit.

Spring is about to leave,
looking back on the radiant years, lingering,
watching the last petals float away as the water flows gently by,
I sit in silence before a bottle of Tender Spring Bamboo, waiting,
waiting for the sky to clear.

憶江南二首

春去也，
多謝洛城人。
弱柳從風疑舉袂，
叢蘭裛露似沾巾。
獨坐亦含嚬。

春去也，
共惜豔陽年。
猶有桃花流水上，
無辭竹葉醉尊前。
惟待見青天。

2

Bai Juyi 白居易
Abiding Love, Xiang Ling 湘靈

Bai Juyi was born in 772, ten years after our superstar, Li Bai, died and two years after the death of Du Fu, our other superstar. Like Du Fu, he came from a scholar-official family, and though his family was not rich either, it was quite a bit better off than Du Fu's. Also, like Du Fu, he was a scholar-official who cared deeply about the country and its people and wrote empathetically about their hardships. As he travelled from post to post and sometimes, in exile, he loved to read his poems to the country folk around him. He famously said that he wanted his poetry to be understandable to old peasant women and children alike. Thus, the words he used are often deceptively simple and sometimes seem repetitious.

Since he lived such a long life (772-846), and was well-known even in his own time, we have many of his poems, which he had copied and distributed among his friends and acquaintants, more than 2,800 all told. Unsurprisingly, each reader will have their own preferences and emphasize different aspects of his life and works. Arthur Waley, one of the first to introduce him to the West, did not even include "Curse of Passion" or the "Pipa Song" in his initial *Translations from the Chinese,* in which Bai Juyi (or *Po Chü-i* as Waley called him) was prominently featured (N.Y.,

MY CHINA IN TANG POETRY

Knopf, 1919). The present super-brief selection is not made in the interest of introducing the best of or the most significant or representative of Bai Juyi, but to give glimpses into the three loves of his life, beginning with his "first love". She was a childhood playmate who became the unreachable star of his life, and who, I find, takes center stage in many of his love poems, and not least, in his best-loved (even in Japan) poem, "Curse of Passion". Secondly, his love of his friend, Yuan Zhen, and thirdly, his love of his people, especially the poor, hard-working country people, of whom his first love, Xiang Ling, was one.

THE NEIGHBOR'S DAUGHTER

> Heaven-sent, almost fifteen, she's just come of age:
> a daytime moon goddess, an early blossoming lotus.
> My parrot tells me she even taught him how to speak.
> She's a painting of a girl embroidering at her window.

> 鄰女

> 娉婷十五勝天仙，
> 白日嫦娥旱地蓮。
> 何處閒教鸚鵡語，
> 碧紗窗下繡牀前。

By the time she was fifteen, he and Xiang Ling had been playmates for eight years. The poem reveals to us his current feelings for her were new to him. Instead of a playmate, she had now become a "moon goddess," a "blooming lotus," "a painting"—all seemingly out of his reach (lotus grows in the middle of a pond), and she even had magical powers, as she taught his parrot how to speak. Here's that parrot mentioned in

FRIENDS AND LOVERS

"A Spring Tune" many years later in the last chapter.

He met her when he was eleven at the little town of Fuli, where his father was serving as an official. He and his mother were moved there from Shanxi to join him and take shelter from the chaos of battle. Xiang Ling was four years his junior and, as Li Bai said of the little Long Pole couple, they "grew up/side by side, strangers to deceit and suspicion". By the time he turned nineteen, he had fallen madly in love with her. "The Neighbor's Daughter" was probably written at this time, when the young couple became aware that their attraction to each other was more than that of playmates. Fifteen was marriageable age for a girl in those days, and he wanted to marry her, but he would have to wait another ten years before he even worked up the courage to ask his mother for permission.

In 808, Bai Juyi turned twenty-seven, went to the capital to take the Imperial Exam required for entry into the life of a courtier or official of the dynasty. Thus, after sixteen years of growing up together and then becoming lovers, he found himself having to leave her, hopefully not for long. He was gone for two years. Here are three of the poems he wrote to or about Xiang Ling during that time.

SENT TO XIANG LING

> Tears on my face have turned to ice on this wintry day. Whenever I'm up here, I cannot help but turn my head towards that distant west tower I left behind, knowing there is someone there, also in misery, alone, waiting.

MY CHINA IN TANG POETRY

寄湘靈

淚眼凌寒凍不流，
每經高處即回頭。
遙知別後西樓上，
應憑欄杆獨自愁。

Xiang Ling 湘靈 is a rather unusual name for a girl from a poor, peasant family. It is the name of the goddess of River Xiang who appeared in "Distant Travels," an ancient poem in the *Chu Ci*, *Songs of the South*, by Qu Yuan or Song Yu, circa 200 BCE. Was there a scholar in this family, poor as they were?

The next poem is a "Forever Longing for Each Other" or "Thinking of You" 長相思 poem. This poem is written in her voice, not an unusual trick for Chinese lovers to use. What is new here, is that the poem begins with what sounds like a shamanistic ritual with all the nines and repetitions and has a fantasy-like ending. In other words, it takes us back to the *Chu Ci* (*Songs of the South*) and the river goddess. Moreover, the promise at the end looks forward to that in the famous "Curse of Passion". In it, he also makes use of the clichéd expression of a person's intestines being tied up in knots to describe misery 斷腸, an equivalent of the English heartbreaking phenomenon to describe the same feeling. He freshens up the cliché, however, by describing the intestines as a rope that winds round the person nine times in misery. In other words, he ties the person up in knots outside instead of inside the body! Just as miserable one imagines. These intestines have given translators no end of trouble and one has to resort to different ways to transport them in different contexts.

About half-way down the poem, the speaker calls him "husband." This either suggests that they had consummated their relationship, or she was depicted as being very forward.

In the poem she claims they met when they were fifteen and were now twenty-three. In actual fact she was only seven when they first met and he, eleven. Perhaps when she was fifteen was when they first became aware that there was sexual attraction between them. In any case, the use of the usnea grass and pine tree images to describe them brings up the low (grass) and high (tree) status of their families which suggests that Bai may have made his intentions known to his mother and the old woman had already objected by bringing up their respective social status and rejected her for not being good enough for her son.

THINKING OF YOU THINKING OF ME

> In the ninth month, fierce west wind rises,
> as the cold moon makes frost flowers in the air.
> Thoughts of you lengthen deep autumn nights,
> my spirit flies to you, nine times high it flies.
> In the second month, the east wind comes,
> splitting branches for leaves and buds to grow.
> Longing for you delayed spring's arrival,
> my misery walks nine circles around me.
> I live on the north side of Tianjin bridge,
> and you live, my husband, on the south.
> When we first met, we were just fifteen,
> eight years have we known each other.
> I am like the usnea grass, growing
> by the side of the tall pine tree, and
> my tassels are too weak to climb up
> the towering pine. But people say if
> we wish hard enough, then Heaven
> will surely make our wish come true.
> I am willing to become a wild beast

MY CHINA IN TANG POETRY

to walk shoulder to shoulder with you.
I am willing to live high on a mountain
and grow with you like vines in the forest.

長相思

九月西風興，月冷霜華凝。
思君秋夜長，一夜魂九升。
二月東風來，草拆花心開。
思君春日遲，一日腸九回。
妾住洛橋北，君住洛橋南。
十五即相識，今年二十三。
有如女蘿草，生在松之側。
蔓短枝苦高，縈迴上不得。
人言人有願，願至天必成。
願作遠方獸，步步比肩行。
願作深山木，枝枝連理生。

Beyond having her address him as "my husband" in the last poem, the poet imagines her in her bedroom in the next two poems and describes spousal activities. All in all, these poems have led commentators to speculate that the two may have consummated their relationship before he left for Chang'an.

IN YOUR COLD BEDROOM

Midnight, your quilt just won't turn warm.
Too tired to rouse yet unable to fall asleep.
Incense has almost burned down to nothing,
tear-soaked, your collar has turned to ice.
Wanting shadows to keep you company,
you kept your lamp lit through the night.

FRIENDS AND LOVERS

寒閨夜

夜半衾裯冷，
孤眠懶未能。
籠香銷盡火，
巾淚滴成冰。
為惜影相伴，
通宵不滅燈。

Pre-reading information for the next poem: Brow-painting is apparently something husbands, especially new husbands, do for wives. Maybe they're especially good at it because they do so much brush calligraphy and some paint? "Leaping Crickets" is a coif. Sometimes women's hair is described as clouds. "Sundrenched Terrace" is in that Song Yu poem about the goddess who lives on Witch Mountain. And of course Witch Mountain clouds are always suggestive.

THINKING OF YOU THINKING OF ME

Brows painted dark,
brows painted light,
"Leaping Crickets" half undone, clouds half-concealing,
you walk up and down in the rain on Sun-drenched Terrace.
Witch Mountain high,
Witch Mountain low,
in the misty, evening rain, waiting for your lover's return,
you are all alone, keeping guard in an empty room. No one comes.

MY CHINA IN TANG POETRY

長相思

深畫眉，
淺畫眉。
蟬鬢鬅鬙雲滿衣，
陽臺行雨回。
巫山高，
巫山低。
暮雨瀟瀟郎不歸，
空房獨守時。

THINKING OF YOU THINKING OF ME

Bian River flows,
Si River flows,
flow to Melon Island's Old Ferry Landing.
My misery is like the mountain ranges of River South.
Thoughts unending,
regrets unending,
regrets will last till I can flow home to you,
under the bright moon, looking out from the high tower.

長相思

汴水流，
泗水流，
流到瓜洲古渡頭。
吳山點點愁。
思悠悠，
恨悠悠，
恨到歸時方始休。
月明人倚樓。

Finally, he passed the *jinshi* exam and received an appointment. Having thus succeeded in obtaining what he came for, he left the capital for home, thinking he had now earned the right to ask his mother for permission to wed and move with his new wife to his place of employment close to Chang'an. By this time, his father had died. He ended up staying in Fuli for ten months, asking and asking his mother for permission to marry Xiang Ling, but the old woman stubbornly refused, for the sole reason, and to her the obvious reason, that Xiang Ling's family was too poor and their status too low for the match to be successful. In the end, Bai Juyi had to reluctantly leave Xiang Ling behind and go report for duty. The First Day of Winter is a rather important festival day, and family members usually try to have dinner together. If one were away from home, he or she would try to return in time for the celebration. Thus, the mention of the festival day in the title implies he viewed her as family, that is, as his wife.

THOUGHTS OF XIANG LING ON THE FIRST NIGHT OF WINTER

> I close my eyes to picture your lovely face,
> but my cold coverlet kept interfering.
> On this longest of all the long nights, I can
> hardly bear thinking of you sleeping all alone.

> 冬至夜懷湘靈

> 艷質無由見,
> 寒衾不可親。
> 何堪最長夜,
> 俱作獨眠人。

MY CHINA IN TANG POETRY

AUTUMN FEELINGS, SENT FROM AFAR

Disheartened, overwhelmed by the season's end,
we are still separated, torn at by the same feelings.
It just won't go away, this heavy knot of sadness,
even autumn wind in the courtyard cannot dispel it.
I see the shadow of the swallow's wing trying to fly.
Orchid fragrance in the old garden stirs my senses.
When can we meet again? When is New Year's Day?
Empty promises, empty and stubbornly unyielding.

感秋寄遠

惆悵時節晚，
兩情千里同。
離憂不散處，
庭樹正秋風。
燕影動歸翼，
蕙香銷故叢。
佳期與芳歲，
牢落兩成空。

LOOKING INTO THE DISTANCE

I would forget but I cannot forget.
I would go but have no reason to go.
I would fly but cannot grow wings.
White hairs have found a way to me.
To sit and watch new falling leaves,
the best place is the highest tower.
Dusk rises to reach the farthest horizon,
and I strain my eyes in miserable pursuit.

FRIENDS AND LOVERS

寄遠

欲忘忘未得，
欲去去無由。
兩腋不生翅，
二毛空滿頭。
坐看新落葉，
行上最高樓。
暝色無邊際，
茫茫盡眼愁。

 Our poet remained unmarried for another ten years. When he turned thirty-seven, his stubbornly unyielding mother threatened suicide if he would not take a Miss Yang for his wife. Miss Yang was a good match, the sister of a friend from their ancestral village. Though Bai Juyi finally gave in to his mother's wishes, he could not forget Xiang Ling. He wrote more poems to express his regret.

NIGHT RAIN

There is one who dwells in my heart,
she lives far away in a distant village.
There are things that hold on to me,
making knots, deep, deep inside me.
The village is far away, I cannot go,
but every day I gaze in that direction.
The deep knots are wound too tightly,
I can't unwind my thoughts from them.
Late into the night, my lamp is going out,
how can I stand this empty, lonely house?
Ahead of autumn, wind and rain arrive,

taking over all our nights and our days.
Not having practiced the way of the ascetic,
can one calmly forget one's past happiness?

夜雨

我有所念人，隔在遠遠鄉。
我有所感事，結在深深腸。
鄉遠去不得，無日不瞻望。
腸深解不得，無夕不思量。
況此殘燈夜，獨宿在空堂。
秋天殊未曉，風雨正蒼蒼。
不學頭陀法，前心安可忘。

Autumn pools are eyes, usually used to describe a woman's eyes. Here, I am using them for his eyes. I have translated lines 3 and 4 together.

THE MIRROR

When she said goodbye to me, my beloved
gave me a box where she had left a mirror.
Since that lovely face like a lotus has gone,
my autumn pool has been deprived of color.
For years I have avoided looking in the box,
and layers of dust have settled on the mirror.
Today I cleaned the mirror and was greeted
by an old man with a withered face. Returning
the mirror to its box, I fell back on my despair.
On the mirror's back are two entwining dragons.

FRIENDS AND LOVERS

感鏡

美人與我別，留鏡在匣中。
自從花顏去，秋水無芙蓉。
經年不開匣，紅埃覆青銅。
今朝一拂拭，自照憔悴容。
照罷重惆悵，背有雙盤龍。

A few months before he married Miss Yang, he was sightseeing with a few friends and passed by the spot where Yang Guifei died. His friends asked him to write a poem about Emperor Xuanzong and his Imperial Consort and how they caused the collapse of his reign. This was how he came to write the "Curse of Passion," better known as "Song of Everlasting Sorrow". This poem was included in Volume I to tell the historical tale and there I have not broken the narrative into sections as I have done here. I have also translated some parts differently but the differences are slight. My purpose of inserting the poem here, coming from his poems to Xiang Ling is to let you hear the echoes of his own "curse of passion". By this time, he knew his longed-for union with her would not come about. His loss is no less painful than that of the Tang Emperor's.

CURSE OF PASSION

The King of Han was a sensual man, bent on winning
his Kingdom's Fall. For years he searched in vain
until one day he found her in the Yang family's care.
Raised in seclusion, the world had yet to set eyes on her.
Such beauty is born of heaven and would not be denied,
and soon she was chosen to take her place by the King's side.
At the turn of her head, a smile, and none escaped her charm.

MY CHINA IN TANG POETRY

Next to her, ladies of all Six Palaces grew pale.
Early in spring he had the Pool of Blossoms prepared:
hot spring water rolled off her creamy flesh like pearls
till half-leaning on palace maids she emerged
Sultry and beguiling, she won the King's heart.

Her hair like clouds, her face like a flower,
her golden steps held sway. Behind lotus bed-curtains
warm nights of spring were spent. Spring nights were short
and mornings hard to catch: the king no longer attended
early audience, his nights were used up in play. Not a day
passed without a celebration, as spring followed spring laughter
and night turned round to night. Three thousand beauties
awaited their lover, his favors for three thousand lavished on one.
For her he fashioned a golden palace, for him she banished night,
when feasts at jade pavilions were over, feasts of passion began.

Her sisters and brothers filled all the high places,
splendid gifts lit up their once humble doors.
Throughout the kingdom parents were saying,
not sons, but daughters, were worth much more.
Above Black Horse Ridges, tall spires pierced purple clouds.
Immortal music drifting through the air reached mortal ears everywhere.
Flow of songs, threads of dance, spun a web of silk and bamboo trance.
All for the king's pleasure, the days were never long enough.
Without warning, war drums of Yu Yang shook the earth.

scattering the dance of "Feather Smocks and Rainbow Skirts."
Outside Ninefold City Gates, smoke and dust rose high,
thousands of carts and horses cluttered the southwest sky.
Imperial banners trembled in the wind, faltering onward,
leaving the capital behind. Only thirty miles out of the city,
all six regiments refused to move on. What could the King do
but grant their wish, the wish of soldiers immune to her
  allure.
She yielded to their call, and reeling before their horses, died.
Her golden headdress fell to the ground for no one to claim.
The king covered his face, knowing he could not save her,
and when he turned to look, blood and tears flowed as one.

The yellow sand would not settle in the biting, soughing wind.
They crossed Twin Blades' hanging bridges, climbing over
  clouds.
Below the cliffs of Moth Brow Ranges there were few
  passersby.
His royal banners had lost their color. The sky had grown dim.
The waters of Shu are green, the mountains of Shu are blue,
the chill of dawn and dusk suffused the monarch's longing.
A cold moon shone on his imperial camp, breaking his heart,
through the night rain a distant bell reminded him of her
  voice.

And the sky rolled round, and the earth came full circle,
and the imperial train returned to the place where his love
  was lost
on the muddy slopes of Ghost Rock. He hesitated to move on.
She lay under this indifferent mud, with nothing to mark the
  spot.

MY CHINA IN TANG POETRY

The king and his ministers looked at each other as tears silently fell.
Turning east to the city gates, they let their horses go where they will.
Returning to the familiar, to the Pond of Lotus Dripping Dew,
to the Evergreen Hall in the Willow's Shade, he saw her face
in the lotus flower, her brows in the willow's yielding branches.
Everywhere he looked she was there. How could his tears not fall?

On nights when spring blossoms were teased open by the wind,
or when, in autumn, the rain fell furiously on wutong trees,
the king lay awake. In his royal residence grass grew wild.
Fallen leaves remained upswept, red petals covered the steps.
Apprentice actors in Pear Garden counted new white hairs,
and ladies-in-waiting in Pepper Rooms watched their hair turn grey.
At nightfall, fireflies and memories stole into the silent corridors,
and in his room, he sat alone, trimming the wick of a dying lamp.
The hour-drum struck early; the long nights persisted.
Stubborn stars struggled to keep the sky from dawning.
Mandarin ducks huddled together in the heavy morning frost.
Who was there to hold the king, to keep his kingfisher quilt warm?
So great the distance that separates the dead from the living,
another year had passed and still her ghost was denied his dreams.

FRIENDS AND LOVERS

A Taoist priest from Lingqiong, a medium who could reach spirits
by his sincerity, was summoned to the capital.
Moved by the king's longing, he agreed to help find her.
Fast as lightning he rode the air, parting clouds,
combing the heavens above and the earth below,
but neither in the rarefied heights of Green Heaven
nor in the nether world of Yellow Spring was there
any trace of her, until a voice from nowhere revealed
that there was a magic mountain far out in the sea,
where pavilions rose like crystals on rainbow clouds,
and among the radiant faces of the immortal beauties,
there was one whose skin was softer than snow and whose face
was like a flower, and she was the one they called Most True.
He arrived then before a golden gate and knocked on the palace door.
Soon, fairy maids appeared one after another to announce his arrival.
Behind Nine Flower bed-curtains she had dreamed the news:
from the House of Han, his messenger had at last come to call.

Startled from her dreams, not quite awake,
she pushed her pillows aside and straightened her robe.
Pearl curtains and silver veils opened one by one:
headdress rumpled, chignon undone, fresh from sleep she came.
The wind played on her sleeves, lifting them, as if
still to the dance of "Feather Smocks and Rainbow Skirts".
Her face like a lone white flower, tears about to fall,
she was like a branch of pear blossoms dressed in spring and rain.

Holding back her tears, she thanked her king for not forgetting her:
"Once parted, the living from the dead, faces, voices, are hard to recall.
Those days at the Morning Sun, when our love seemed eternal,
are not as long as the endless days here in eternal heaven.
Each time I turn to look on the circle-of-dust below,
I see only a veil of mist covering the capital, Chang'an.
All I have are these objects now to convey my feelings.
Here is a gold casket and a golden hairpin too, take one side each of these treasures and let them speak of our love.
If our hearts can learn their lessons, like gold we will endure,
and the day will come when the sky above will meet the earth below."

As the priest took his leave, she repeated her words more urgently,
and in her words, she hid a promise that only their two hearts knew.
On the Seventh Day of the Seventh Month, at the Palace of Eternity,
in the middle of the night, they whispered to each other this private vow:
we'll fly in the air like those fabulous birds who share one pair of wings,
we'll grow from the earth like twin branches out of the self-same tree.
The sky is long, the earth is old, but in time they too will end.
Our unfinished web of passion will spin till time is spent.

FRIENDS AND LOVERS

長恨歌

漢皇重色思傾國，禦宇多年求不得。
楊家有女初長成，養在深閨人未識。
天生麗質難自棄，一朝選在君王側。
回眸一笑百媚生，六宮粉黛無顏色。
春寒賜浴華清池，溫泉水滑洗凝脂。
侍兒扶起嬌無力，始是新承恩澤時。
雲鬢花顏金步搖，芙蓉帳暖度春宵。
春宵苦短日高起，從此君王不早朝。
承歡侍宴無閒暇，春從春遊夜專夜。
後宮佳麗三千人，三千寵愛在一身。
金屋妝成嬌侍夜，玉樓宴罷醉和春。
姊妹弟兄皆列土，可憐光彩生門戶。
遂令天下父母心，不重生男重生女。
驪宮高處入青雲，仙樂風飄處處聞。
緩歌慢舞凝絲竹，盡日君王看不足。
漁陽鼙鼓動地來，驚破霓裳羽衣曲。
九重城闕煙塵生，千乘萬騎西南行。
翠華搖搖行復止，西出都門百餘里。
六軍不發無奈何，宛轉蛾眉馬前死。
花鈿委地無人收，翠翹金雀玉搔頭。
君王掩面救不得，回看血淚相和流。
黃埃散漫風蕭索，雲棧縈紆登劍閣。
峨嵋山下少人行，旌旗無光日色薄。
蜀江水碧蜀山青，聖主朝朝暮暮情。
行宮見月傷心色，夜雨聞鈴腸斷聲。
天旋地轉回龍馭，到此躊躇不能去。
馬嵬坡下泥土中，不見玉顏空死處。
君臣相顧盡沾衣，東望都門信馬歸。
歸來池苑皆依舊，太液芙蓉未央柳。
芙蓉如面柳如眉，對此如何不淚垂？
春風桃李花開日，秋雨梧桐葉落時。

MY CHINA IN TANG POETRY

西宮南內多秋草，落葉滿階紅不掃。
梨園弟子白髮新，椒房阿監青娥老。
夕殿螢飛思悄然，孤燈挑盡未成眠。
遲遲鐘鼓初長夜，耿耿星河欲曙天。
鴛鴦瓦冷霜華重，翡翠衾寒誰與共？
悠悠生死別經年，魂魄不曾來入夢。
臨邛道士鴻都客，能以精誠致魂魄。
為感君王輾轉思，遂教方士殷勤覓。
排空馭氣奔如電，昇天入地求之遍。
上窮碧落下黃泉，兩處茫茫皆不見。
忽聞海上有仙山，山在虛無縹緲間。
樓閣玲瓏五雲起，其中綽約多仙子。
中有一人字太真，雪膚花貌參差是。
金闕西廂叩玉扃，轉教小玉報雙成。
聞道漢家天子使，九華帳裏夢魂驚。
攬衣推枕起徘徊，珠箔銀屏迤邐開。
雲鬢半偏新睡覺，花冠不整下堂來。
風吹仙袂飄飄舉，猶似霓裳羽衣舞。
玉容寂寞淚闌干，梨花一枝春帶雨。
含情凝睇謝君王，一別音容兩渺茫。
昭陽殿裏恩愛絕，蓬萊宮中日月長。
回頭下望人寰處，不見長安見塵霧。
惟將舊物表深情，鈿合金釵寄將去。
釵留一股合一扇，釵擘黃金合分鈿。
但教心似金鈿堅，天上人間會相見。
臨別殷勤重寄詞，詞中有誓兩心知。
七月七日長生殿，夜半無人私語時。
在天願作比翼鳥，在地願為連理枝。
天長地久有時盡，此恨綿綿無絕期。

Miss Yang turned out to be a good wife, and the poem Bai Juyi composed to give her some guidance turned out to be quite unnecessary. To our modern eyes, this wedding gift is somewhat amusing.

A GIFT FOR MY WIFE

In life we shall live close together in one room.
In death we shall be laid side by side in the earth.
My friends often give me support and advice,
it is only to be expected that I do the same for you.
Qian Lou[6] stubbornly stuck to his vow of poverty,
and his virtuous wife forgot how hard it is to be poor.
Ji Que[7] was a farmer who treated his wife with respect,
and she, for her part, treated him like an honoured guest.
Tao Qian refused to bow just to earn a living,
his wife happily chopped wood to keep them warm.
Liang Hong also refused to serve and agreed to marry
Meng Guang because she chose coarse cotton over silk.
Even though you have not read many books,
you must have heard of these virtuous people.[8]
After all these thousands of years, they have left
stories to show us how we should live our lives.

---

6   Qian Lou was a recluse who lived during the Warring States Period. Despite many visits by kings for him to come out of poverty and serve at court, he refused, because he did not want to live comfortably in luxury while he sees how wretched poor people lived.
7   Ji Que lived during the Spring and Autumn Period (770-476 BCE).
8   Liang Hung and Meng Guang are from the later Han Dynasty (25-220 CE). As the story goes, Liang Hong was a virtuous man and had a great reputation but refused to marry the wives that were offered him. Meng Guang was very ugly, fat, and strong, she, too, had many offers of marriage, because her family was very rich. She, however, rejected everyone and proposed to marry Liang Hong because of his virtue. He said yes, but for seven days after their wedding he refused to speak to her or even look at her. She went down on her knees to ask him why, and he said it was because her clothes were too fancy! He said, "I married you because I thought you were a virtuous woman and married me because of my honesty." She said, of course, I have also prepared coarse cotton clothes to wear, and discarded all her silks. At which point, they lived contentedly together. A few years later, she suggested they fulfill his promise to become a recluse and live far away from the city and her family's wealth and be self-sufficient for the rest of their lives.

MY CHINA IN TANG POETRY

So long as we are trapped in this earthly existence,
we cannot forget to take good care of our bodies,
but all we need are simple clothes on our back
and enough food in our bellies. We have no need
for riches or elegant clothing or extravagant feasts.
Thick socks to keep our feet warm in the winter
is all we want; fancy embroideries are not required.
You have been brought up with good family values,
and understand the importance of a clean reputation.
I am a long-suffering man who asks no more than that.
This marriage is a new beginning for both you and me.
For the sake of generations to come, let us stay poor
and honest and be content with our lives till the end.

贈內

生為同室親，死為同穴塵。
他人尚相勉，而況我與君。
黔婁固窮士，妻賢忘其貧。
冀缺一農夫，妻敬儼如賓。
陶潛不營生，翟氏自爨薪。
梁鴻不肯仕，孟光甘布裙。
君雖不讀書，此事耳亦聞。
至此千載後，傳是何如人。
人生未死間，不能忘其身。
所須者衣食，不過飽與溫。
蔬食足充饑，何必膏粱珍。
繒絮足禦寒，何必錦繡文。
君家有貽訓，清白遺子孫。
我亦貞苦士，與君新結婚。
庶保貧與素，偕老同欣欣。

How would you like to marry him?

    As the story goes, around 815, when Bai Juyi offended the authorities and was banished to Xun Yang, he and his wife ran into Xiang Ling and her father, on the banks of a river, quite likely the Pen River in "Pipa Song" below. She had remained unmarried. If the dating is correct, he would have been forty-three and his old flame thirty-nine, considered old and past their prime. There, they seemed to have reminisced and "held each other's head and cried bitterly," as the saying goes. In any case, Bai wrote the following poems after they said good-bye.

ON SEEING YOU AGAIN (two poems)

> I combed back my white hair to find new misery.
> Your painted moth-brows cannot hide your age.
> Others think it odd, to see us sad at this reunion.
> Separated in youth, we meet again as old people.
>
> It has been a long time since we were together.
> It took me a while to believe this is not a dream.
> This should be a happy event, even if, in the end,
> after our cups are emptied, all is naught again.

> 逢舊 (二首)
> 我梳白髮添新恨，
> 君掃青娥減舊容。
> 應被傍人怪惆悵，
> 少年離別老相逢。

MY CHINA IN TANG POETRY

久別偶相逢，
俱疑是夢中。
即今歡樂事，
放盞又成空。

And yes, his wife was supposed to be right there with them. A year later, he wrote the "Pipa Song".

PIPA SONG

Prologue
It was in the tenth year of Yuan Ho [815] that I was demoted and banished to the County of Nine Waters. The next autumn, I was seeing off a friend at Xunyang's river mouth of Pen. Through the darkness came the sound of someone playing the pipa, so lively the sound, it reminded me of the capital. We requested a meeting and found out that she had once been a singing girl in Chang'an and studied under Master Mu and Master Cao. As she grew older and her beauty faded, she married herself to a merchant. I called for more wine and asked for a few tunes. At the end of her song, she reminisced about the happy days of her youth and how she came to be drifting on these desolate waters. It had been two years since I left the capital, and I thought I had learned to be content, but her words stirred in me once again the pain of exile. That night, I wrote this poem of eighty-eighty lines as a gift to her, calling it "Pipa Song".

> Late one evening I came to see off a friend at the river mouth of Pen:
> maples and bulrushes quivered in the desolate darkness as I dismounted.
> We started to drink and say goodbye, wishing for music to

FRIENDS AND LOVERS

    ease our pain,
as the moon sank lower and lower into the water.
Drunk yet not happy how could I let him go?
Suddenly, out of the water came notes of a pipa.
I forgot about going and my friend stayed on.
Where did it come from? Who was playing?
The music stopped but no answer came.
I called for more wine, had candles relit,
and prepared to resume our farewell dinner.
We paddled closer to ask for a meeting.
Countless calls, more pleading, she finally came out,
still carrying the pipa, half-covering her face.[9]
As she tuned, turning pegs and strumming strings,
melody yet to come, feelings flowed through.
Her playing was calm, her singing composed,
but together they told of a whole life's wrongs.
Lowered brows, sure hands, telling all,
endless memories of the deep heart's core.
Combing, spinning, ripple and *pick*,[10]
first "Rainbow Skirts," then "The Green Waist":
thick strings came crashing like rapid rain,
thin strings came cooing like intimate words,
crashing, cooing, clashed and merged,
like pearls great and small falling on jade platters.
As the twitter of orioles slid off flowers,
underground water rolled onto the shore.
In the frozen spring water, her music paused,
as if trapped in regret, unable to move on.
Bitterness swelled in the ghostly stillness,

---

9   The pipa is generally played in an upright position, which is why it is half-covering her face.
10 These are technical terms familiar to pipa players.

MY CHINA IN TANG POETRY

this moment's silence surpassing sound.
Then, from a silver vessel bursting open,
iron riders charged out, clanging swords.
The song ended with a slash across the heart:
four strings, one voice, like tearing silk.
East boat, west boat, all was still.
An autumn moon darted white on the river.
Hesitating as she put her instrument down,
she straightened her dress, composed herself
and said, "I have come from the capital
and once lived at the foot of Xia Ma.
By thirteen I had mastered the pipa, coming
first in my class at the Imperial Academy.
Every tune I played the experts applauded,
and my beauty was the envy of all the girls.
Young men from Wu Ling poured in with gifts,
one song brought in rolls and rolls of red silk.
Gold combs and silver pins jingled in rhythmic sway
and blood-red silk skirts were stained with spilt wine.
One year's laughter tumbled into the next:
autumn moons, spring winds, slipped away.
Then, my brother left with the army and my aunt died.
Dusk went, dawn came, those colours remained,
but at my front door, carts and horses stopped no more.
No longer young, I became wife to a merchant.
Profit means more to him than staying with me.
Last month he went off to Fu Liang to buy tea,
leaving me in this empty boat at the river's mouth.
Around my boat the moon is bright, the water cold,
and deep in the night dreams of my youth return to me,
those days of rouge dreams still flood my eyes".
On hearing the pipa tell I had sighed,

FRIENDS AND LOVERS

now hearing her story I'm caught once more.
Castaways, we drift together and part again,
I know you well without knowing you at all.
Since taking leave of the capital last year
I have been an exile, bedridden at Xun Yang.
Xun Yang is barren country, no music
all year round, no sound of string or pipe.
I live in the damp lowland of the Pen River,
yellow reeds, bitter bamboos, grow round my house.
From dawn to dusk, what do I hear?
The cuckoo spitting blood and the gibbon's shrieks.
By spring rivers at morning and on autumn moon nights
I drink by myself and pour for myself.
Mountain ballads and village flutes there are,
but their crude clattering is hard to bear.
Tonight, as your pipa spoke to me
like ethereal music, my senses cleared.
Don't go, please sit, and play another tune,
and I'll write a poem for your pipa song.
Deeply moved, she pondered my offer,
then sat once more and ran the strings, pulling fast,
faster, yet chillier than the tune before.
Everyone secretly wiped their eyes,
and who among them wept the most?
This petty official's coarse robe was soaked.

MY CHINA IN TANG POETRY

琵琶行

元和十年，予左遷九江郡司馬。明年秋，送客湓浦口，聞舟中夜彈琵琶者，聽其音，錚錚然有京都聲。問其人，本長安倡女，嘗學琵琶於穆、曹二善才，年長色衰，委身為賈人婦。遂命酒，使快彈數曲。曲罷憫然，自敘少小時歡樂事，今漂淪憔悴，轉徙於江湖間。予出官二年，恬然自安，感斯人言，是夕始覺有遷謫意。因為長句，歌以贈之，凡六百一十六言，命曰《琵琶行》。

潯陽江頭夜送客，楓葉荻花秋瑟瑟。
主人下馬客在船，舉酒欲飲無管絃。
醉不成歡慘將別，別時茫茫江浸月。
忽聞水上琵琶聲，主人忘歸客不發。
尋聲闇問彈者誰，琵琶聲停欲語遲。
移船相近邀相見，添酒回燈重開宴。
千呼萬喚始出來，猶抱琵琶半遮面。
轉軸撥絃三兩聲，未成曲調先有情。
絃絃掩抑聲聲思，似訴平生不得志。
低眉信手續續彈，說盡心中無限事。
輕攏慢撚抹復挑，初為霓裳後六么。
大絃嘈嘈如急雨，小絃切切如私語。
嘈嘈切切錯雜彈，大珠小珠落玉盤。
間關鶯語花底滑，幽咽泉流水下灘。
水泉冷澀絃凝絕，凝絕不通聲暫歇。
別有幽愁闇恨生，此時無聲勝有聲。
銀瓶乍破水漿迸，鐵騎突出刀槍鳴。
曲終收撥當心畫，四絃一聲如裂帛。
東船西舫悄無言，唯見江心秋月白。
沉吟放撥插絃中，整頓衣裳起斂容。
自言本是京城女，家在蝦蟆陵下住。
十三學得琵琶成，名屬教坊第一部。
曲罷曾教善才服，妝成每被秋娘妒。

FRIENDS AND LOVERS

五陵年少爭纏頭，一曲紅綃不知數。
鈿頭銀篦擊節碎，血色羅裙翻酒污。
今年歡笑復明年，秋月春風等閒度。
弟走從軍阿姨死，暮去朝來顏色故。
門前冷落車馬稀，老大嫁作商人婦。
商人重利輕別離，前月浮梁買茶去。
去來江口守空船，繞船月明江水寒。
夜深忽夢少年事，夢啼妝淚紅闌干。
我聞琵琶已歎息，又聞此語重唧唧。
同是天涯淪落人，相逢何必曾相識。
我從去年辭帝京，謫居臥病潯陽城。
潯陽地僻無音樂，終歲不聞絲竹聲。
住近湓江地低溼，黃蘆苦竹繞宅生。
其間旦暮聞何物，杜鵑啼血猿哀鳴。
春江花朝秋月夜，往往取酒還獨傾。
豈無山歌與村笛，嘔啞嘲哳難為聽。
今夜聞君琵琶語，如聽仙樂耳暫明。
莫辭更坐彈一曲，為君翻作琵琶行。
感我此言良久立，卻坐促絃絃轉急。
悽悽不似向前聲，滿座重聞皆掩泣。
座中泣下誰最多？江州司馬青衫濕。

3

Love of Folk and Country

Together with his best friend, Yuan Zhen, Bai Juyi was promoting the New Music Bureau Movement, the *xin yue fu yun dong,* 新樂府運動, a revival in folk interests promoted by Du Fu before them. The Music Bureau genre itself was not new; it had existed since the Han dynasty, centuries ago. Music Bureau refers to a government agency in charge of collecting folk songs and poems, recognized as important to the culture since Confucius (551-479 BCE), who had collected them for the *Book of Songs* 詩經 *Shijing*, and called folk songs "the voice of the people". The later *yuefu* poems are mostly imitations of such folk material. With the Tang poets, this was a conscientious effort to "make it new". Basically, they are poetry of the people, from the people. Yuan and Bai who promoted the movement in mid-Tang, prescribed using easy to understand language and material current or relevant to improving people's lives.

The most famous of Bai Juyi's *yuefu* poems are the two long poems we have already seen, "Curse of Passion" and "Pipa Song". These are relevant to "the present" because one is an admonition (do not behave like "the sensual man" who almost lost his kingdom), even though it ended up being more moving as a love poem, and the latter poem is a narrative in sympathy with the aging pipa player, even if it ended up being also about the banished poet himself. The next two famous *yuefu* narratives are "The Charcoal Vender at South Mountain," and "Watching a Harvest", and the political comment here is obvious.

THE CHARCOAL VENDER AT SOUTH MOUNTAIN

His face is the colour of fiery smoke and heated dust.
His grey hair is blackened, his fingers burnt to soot.
How much can he get for a load of charcoal you ask.
Just enough for food in his belly, and a rag on his back.
Pitifully thin are the clothes on his body, yet still he
wishes for a cold winter to drive up the price of coal.
Overnight snow fell a whole foot deep. Early the next
morning he braves snow and sleet and heads for the city.
The ox is tired, the man is hungry, and the sun has risen high.
South of the city gate, he parks by the roadside to take a rest.
And who should come along but two handsome horsemen,
one in the court's yellow satin and his follower, in white.
He pulls out an official-looking document and reads out loud,
claiming possession of the load. Feebly, the vendor looks on,
as the riders pull his cart away and head back north, leaving
half a roll of red gauze and a short length of silk draped over
his old bull's head: a fair price for his half-burnt wood!

MY CHINA IN TANG POETRY

賣炭翁
伐薪燒炭南山中

滿面塵灰煙火色，兩鬢蒼蒼十指黑。
賣炭得錢何所營？身上衣裳口中食。
可憐身上衣正單，心憂炭賤願天寒。
夜來城上一尺雪，曉駕炭車輾冰轍。
牛困人飢日已高，市南門外泥中歇。
翩翩兩騎來是誰，黃衣使者白衫兒。
手把文書口稱敕，迴車叱牛牽向北。
一車炭，千餘斤，宮使驅將惜不得。
半匹紅紗一丈綾，繫向牛頭充炭直。

WATCHING A HARVEST

Farmers have few idle months,
and the fifth month is their busiest.
When wind rises from the south, overnight,
wheat will turn yellow, covering the fields.
Women come delivering baskets of rice,
children help carry flasks full of soup.
The menfolk stop to gulp down their meals.
Here in the south, the sun burns the earth.
Barefoot, with flame on their shoulders,
they work without a thought to the heat,
making most of the summer's sunlit hours.
Then I noticed one of the peasant women
by her husband's side, an infant on one arm,
and picking grains fallen on the ground,
saving them in an old basket she carried.
Overhearing her conversation with the others
broke my heart. With the heavy taxes owed,

they had to sell their farm, and these few grains will be all they have to stave off hunger for a while. What good deeds have I done in my previous life to deserve this fortune of not being a farmer? Every year I am allotted three hundred *dan* of rice,[11] and by year's end I have rice left over in my granary. This thought clouded my mind with shame, and long into the night, I could not forget her words.

觀刈麥

田家少閒月，五月人倍忙。
夜來南風起，小麥覆隴黃。
婦姑荷簞食，童稚攜壺漿，
相隨餉田去，丁壯在南岡。
足蒸暑土氣，背灼炎天光，
力盡不知熱，但惜夏日長。
復有貧婦人，抱子在其旁，
右手秉遺穗，左臂懸敝筐。
聽其相顧言，聞者為悲傷。
家田輸稅盡，拾此充飢腸。
今我何功德，曾不事農桑。
吏祿三百石，歲晏有餘糧。
念此私自愧，盡日不能忘。

The next few short poems are either about folk life or about living as one of the country people. You may notice that even with these shorter poems, they are much looser or freer than the *lushi*. In fact, even though he still tends to write in five- or seven-character lines, he has occasionally written in lines of three, four,

---

11 One "*dan*" written as 石/擔 = 120 *jin* 斤 or cattie. One cattie =0.6 kilogram, so 300 dan = 3600 kilograms/year.

six, or even eight characters. Also, the number of lines is not prescribed. The following three are all *jueju*s.

Water chestnut leaves are small and float on the water surface. Lotus leaves are large and grow out of the water, sometimes as tall as several meters, thus one can even row boats under them to go from A to B. Look at pictures of them in Chinese lakes and ponds.

SONG OF PICKING LOTUS SEEDS

Water chestnut leaves bobbing up and down on the waves,
under the swaying lotus leaves two small boats meet.
Seeing your lover, you look down, suppressing a smile,
inadvertently letting a jade comb slip and fall in the water.

採蓮曲

菱葉縈波荷颭風，
荷花深處小船通。
逢郎欲語低頭笑，
碧玉搔頭落水中。

NIGHT AT THE VILLAGE

Frost on chilly grass chilly, cold worms chirp, chirping.
South of the village, north of the village, no one around.
I stepped out the front door to gaze on the buckwheat fields:
little white flowers spread out in rows like columns of snow.

FRIENDS AND LOVERS

村夜

霜草蒼蒼蟲切切，
村南村北行人絕。
獨出前門望野田，
月明蕎麥花如雪。

NIGHT SNOW

I was alarmed that my bedding felt so icy cold,
when light came shimmering through the window.
It was snow, of course, falling deep into the night,
snow so heavy that bamboo stalks are crackling.

夜雪

已訝衾枕冷，
復見窗戶明。
夜深知雪重，
時聞折竹聲。

A *fu* 賦 is often translated as "rhapsody," and is an old form of poetry that could be described as something between an essay and a poem. This *fu* is a different character and in a different tone from the *fu* 府 in *yuefu* 樂府 and means something entirely different. I sometimes translate it as an ode because an ode is also used in praise of something or written on a topic in English. It is often set as an exam question, for example, "Write an ode to or on something," and one is given a topic. In this case, the young Bai was given the topic "Seeing off a Friend at the Ancient Grass Plain". He was sixteen, and this poem, when it started circulating, started to make a name for him. Later, the poem became so well-known that it was mostly referred to simply as "Grass". The first six lines might be called "In Praise of Grass" or "Ode to Grass". He then used the couplet at the end to wrap it all up and fulfilled the requirement of the topic, which is "seeing off a friend".

SEEING OFF A FRIEND AT THE ANCIENT GRASS PLAIN

> Green, green the green grass grows:
> a new year, a new crop comes and goes.
> Wildfires may burn it, but it will not die.
> Spring wind blows, and it comes alive.
> Its fragrance breaches ancient highways.
> Its liveliness splashes across old ruins.
> Again, I say to you, farewell, my friend,
> as we gulp down the sorrows of parting.

> 賦得古原草送別
>
> 離離原上草，
> 一歲一枯榮。
> 野火燒不盡，
> 春風吹又生。
> 遠芳侵古道，
> 晴翠接荒城。
> 又送王孫去，
> 萋萋滿別情。

Next comes three poems written on various occasions.

Green ants refer to the fermentation in the wine, so called because they swarm to the bottom of the bottle when first poured. Rice wine is often drunk warmed. This numbering of the brothers in a family can get pretty numerous as often, all the brothers' sons are lined up in this way.

QUESTION FOR BROTHER LIU NINETEEN

Green ants have floated to the top of my newly brewed,
and my red earthen pot is already warming on the stove.
It looks like the sky wants to drop some snow tonight,
how about you come over and share a cup of wine with me?

問劉十九

綠蟻新醅酒,
紅泥小火爐。
晚來天欲雪,
能飲一杯無?

PEACH FLOWERS AT GREAT FOREST SACRED BUDDHIST SHRINE

It's the fourth month of the year, all flowers have fallen.
Here, in this mountain shrine, peach buds are blooming.
Earthlings often ask where flowers go after the spring,
now I have my answer for them: they've all come here!

大林寺桃花

人間四月芳菲盡,
山寺桃花始盛開。
長恨春歸無覓處,
不知轉入此中來。

MY CHINA IN TANG POETRY

MID-AUTUMN FESTIVAL MOON GAZING AT THE KIOSK BY THE PEN RIVER

Written at Nine Waters during exile.

Last year, on Full Moon Night I was at at Imperial Park by Crooked Lake.
This year, on Full Moon Night I am on the sandy banks of Pen River.
Looking West to the North, I am uncertain where my hometown lies.
Gazing East to the South, how many full moons away must I endure?
Last night the wind rose suddenly, but who can tell me what it means?
Tonight, the bright moon shines clear like it used to in years gone by.

八月十五日夜湓亭望月

昔年八月十五夜，
曲江池畔杏園邊。
今年八月十五夜，
湓浦沙頭水館前。
西北望鄉何處是，
東南見月幾回圓。
昨風一吹無人會，
今夜清光似往年。

In 820, Bai was finally reprieved and allowed to go back to the capital, two years later, he was made Governor of Hangzhou, and then in 825, Governor of Suzhou. He retired only a year after the second governorship, due to illness. These were both beautiful areas of the country, and he wrote many poems about the countryside.

Qian Tang Lake in the next poem is the old name for West Lake. West Lake is so named because it lies west of the place called Qian Tang. Jia is the man who built the pagoda named after him. West Lake appears often in Chinese poetry; it is a beautiful scenic attraction.

A WALK BY QIAN TANG LAKE

North of Solitary Mountain Temple, south of Jia's Pagoda,
the lake is calm, holding clouds on its surface like a bowl.
Here and there, early warblers jostle for the warmest branches.
Whose house have the swallows come from looking for mud?
Dizzying colours, flowers flying, falling, bewildering the eye.
New grass has grown just tall enough to cover horses' hooves.
My favourite spot is east of the lake, I can walk here forever,
in the green shade of willows along its White Sand Bridge.

錢塘湖春行

孤山寺北賈亭西，
水面初平雲腳低。
幾處早鶯爭暖樹，
誰家新燕啄春泥。
亂花漸欲迷人眼，
淺草才能沒馬蹄。
最愛湖東行不足，
綠楊陰裏白沙堤.

MY CHINA IN TANG POETRY

Speaking of swallows, here's another Bai Juyi poem that "old peasant women and little children" can read. It is said that the governor can often be seen reading poems to old peasants or children to make sure he got it right. "Swallow Song" is a poem many Chinese children have learned at school. I had always thought in my youth that it was an admonishment to young people to take care of their old parents, a central Confucian precept. Then, when I read it again in college, I saw that the poem was addressed to an old man, a friend of Bai's whose son had left home, not sure for what reason, which gave the poem quite a different point of view. The poem took me many years to translate partly because of the word *liang* 梁, for which I had not been able to dredge up an English name. The other thing that held me up for years, was its fluent simplicity, which is one of the main challenges of translating Bai Juyi generally. His style is easy but not so easy that it becomes flat, and translations of these poems must avoid becoming prose.

"Summer-tree," summer or summer beam is an architectural term that describes any large timber or beam which serves as a bearing surface. I am using it here to refer to the large horizontal beam across the ceiling of old Chinese houses which often have an open sitting room, like a large porch which looks onto the garden or courtyard. Many martial arts movies feature this kind of house. There is a good example of this at the beginning of *Crouching Tiger, Hidden Dragon*.

Here are two versions of the same poem, one with and one without the poet's note after the title. Does it make a difference in your reading? Also, the first one is pretty much line for line, while the second collapses two lines into one. The conclusions to the two versions are also slightly different. The whole Chinese title reads "Swallow Poem Written as Reminder to Old Liu."

FRIENDS AND LOVERS

SWALLOW SONG

For Old Liu who was saddened when his beloved son left home without telling him, just as he himself did when he left his own parents. This made him sad and bitter. I wrote the following poem to remind him of this fact.

> Round about my summer tree,
> two swallows came a-courting,
> bringing mud to build their nest,
> till four chicks to them were born.
> Day and night the four chicks grew,
> chirp, chirp, chirping for worms.
> But worms are not easy to find
> and young mouths don't stop asking.
> All day long, they pecked and clawed
> as if they'd forgotten how to rest.
> Back and forth and back and forth
> and still she wanted to give them more.
> Thirty days and thirty nights,
> the chicks grew fat, the mother thin.
> Tweet, tweet, they learned to speak,
> as she preened their feathers one by one.
> Then, one day, their wings were ready.
> She led them out to the garden tree.
> They took to the wind without a glance
> back to the parents they left behind.
> Mother bird, and father too, called and
> called till darkness filled the empty sky.
> The pair came back to the empty nest,
> keening, weeping through the night.

MY CHINA IN TANG POETRY

O swallow, swallow don't you cry,
remember that day so long gone by,
when, in your youth, you flew away
ever higher, leaving them behind,
then it was they who longed for you,
now you know what longing means.

Alternate Version:

SWALLOW SONG

Round about my summer-tree, a pair of swallows came a-courting,
bringing mud to build their nest, till four chicks to them were born.
Day by day the four chicks grew, chirp, chirp, chirping for worms,
but worms are not easy to find, and young mouths never stop asking.
All day long, they pecked and clawed as if they'd forgotten how to rest.
Back and forth and back and forth, still they wanted to give them more.
Thirty days and thirty nights, the chicks grew fat, the mother thin.
Twit, twit, they learned to speak, as she groomed them one by one.
Then, one day, their wings were ready. She led them to the garden tree.
They took to the wind without a glance back to the pair they left behind.
Mother and father birds, called till darkness filled the empty

sky.
Parent birds came back to an empty nest, keening, weeping in the night.
O swallow, swallow don't you cry, remember that day so long gone by,
when you flew away without a thought for the mother you left behind.
Now you know what it's like to hope and fret with a parent's heart.

燕詩示劉叟

叟有愛子，背叟逃去，叟甚悲念之。叟少年時，亦嘗如是。故作《燕詩》以諭之矣。

梁上有雙燕，翩翩雄與雌。
銜泥兩椽間，一巢生四兒。
四兒日夜長，索食聲孜孜。
青蟲不易捕，黃口無飽期。
嘴爪雖欲敝，心力不知疲。
須臾十來往，猶恐巢中飢。
辛勤三十日，母瘦雛漸肥。
喃喃教言語，一一刷毛衣。
一旦羽翼長，引上庭樹枝。
舉翅不回顧，隨風四散飛。
雌雄空中鳴，聲盡呼不歸，
卻入空巢裏，啁啾終夜悲。
燕燕爾勿悲，爾當反自思，
思爾為雛日，高飛背母時。
當時父母念，今日爾應知。

MY CHINA IN TANG POETRY

Let's end this chapter with another of Bai Juyi's famous poems, this time, during war and separation from his extended family. In writing about his own family, he is also expressing the tragedy of the common man.

Some pre-reading information: Large Chinese families count all male offspring in order of their birth, i.e. brothers' sons, as brothers. Bai's seventh brother is his uncle's son, and the fifteenth probably also a cousin. "Bone and blood" 骨肉 together mean siblings or family members in Chinese; that is the idea behind line 4 here. Without knowing it, they were referring to their DNA! Also, the "five disparate places" in the last line of the poem would be referring to the five places named in the prologue. What I have translated as "one family" in the penultimate line comes from the Chinese expression, "hometown heart" 鄉心, which is in the last line of Bai's poem. The Mid-Autumn Festival, Harvest Moon in the West, is another important festival day when the moon is especially large and bright when it is not clouded over. Chinese families gather to celebrate the moon; the occasion is actually called "Admiring the Moon". In the old days, extended families live under the same roof, or at least close by. When family members are separated, they gaze at the moon and think of each other.

UPON GAZING AT THE MID-AUTUMN MOON

Prologue: Since chaos struck Henan, and famine plagued Guan'nei, my family is scattered, brothers separated. Seeing the autumn moon tonight, I thought of them and sent this poem to my eldest brother at Fouliang, my seventh brother at Yuqian, my fifteenth brother at Wujiang, and family members at Fuli and those in Xiagui.

FRIENDS AND LOVERS

Times are hard, years fallow, homesteads turned inside out:
siblings scattered in all directions, living in make-shift camps,
fields and gardens ravaged, patches of butchered earth.
Bones torn from blood; households spilled onto highways.
Lone geese separated from their flocks, call in the empty sky.
Families thrown about like tumbleweed in the autumn wind.
Tonight, the moon is especially bright, teasing tears. We are one
family, gazing at the same festival moon, in five different places.

望月有感

自河南經亂，關內阻饑，兄弟離散，各在一處。因望月有感，聊書所懷，寄上浮梁大兄、於潛七兄、烏江十五兄，兼示符離及下邽弟妹。

時難年荒世業空，
弟兄羈旅各西東。
田園寥落干戈後，
骨肉流離道路中。
弔影分為千里雁，
辭根散作九秋蓬。
共看明月應垂淚，
一夜鄉心五處同。

4

Yuan-Bai's Friendship

SONG WITHOUT A NAME
Two versions:

Flowers hide in flowers.
Mist disappears in mist.
It comes at midnight,
and goes with dawn.
Like a spring dream it stays but for a while,
like morning clouds, it leaves without a trace.

Flower that's not a flower.
Mist that's not misty.
At night it comes.
At dawn it leaves.
Coming like a spring dream, but for how long?
Leaving like sad clouds, nowhere to be found.

FRIENDS AND LOVERS

花非花

花非花，
霧非霧。
夜半來，
天明去。
來如春夢不多時，
去似朝雲無覓處。

What is this mysterious thing that cannot be named, cannot be detained, cannot be traced? It sounds like something forbidden. Or impossible? Or cannot be realized? Some say this is a poem Bai Juyi wrote for Xiang Ling. Some say it is for Yuan Zhen. And some say it is written for some mistress or other, or even a "singing girl." Also, in those days, officials were all given a certain number of "maids". These maids can be assigned any number of duties, including bedroom duties. Good masters are discreet, so, this sneaking in and out at night is plausible. Or it could be a courtesan or a nun he met and fell for during his travels. In any case, it is a love poem. In any case, it sounds like a tryst. Whatever it was, it was a secret, a private matter. This private matter, moreover, is reminiscent of the story of the Witch Mountain goddess who came to the ancient King of Chu as "cloud in the morning and rain at night" in Song Yu's fairytale that has been told over and over again in these Tang poems. Bai's poem, and it is also made into a song years later, has been recited or sung by many a young romantic ever since.

As mentioned earlier, Bai Juyi met Yuan Zhen the year they passed the *jinshi* exam. Yuan was seven years his junior, but, with their many interests in common, they hit it off right away. As fate would have it, they were assigned to the same post in the same place near the capital for their first appointment. The job was

MY CHINA IN TANG POETRY

not terribly demanding. They were sort of provincial scholars with titles of librarian and editor of official documents. The two did everything together, drinking, playing chess, making music, wandering the countryside, visiting houses of pleasure, writing, answering each other's poems, and composing official petitions together. Eventually, they started the poetic school of the New Music Bureau Movement together. By his own admission, Bai did not make friends easily, so meeting Yuan, a "person who knows me," must have been like finding a companion, maybe even superior to Xiang Ling, because he was a scholar and a poet. There are even stories of them sharing "singing girls". One time, Yuan Zhen even "borrowed" one of Bai's for a whole month. The two were to become lifelong friends, even though they would both be exiled or posted to different parts of the country at some time or other after these first few years. Perhaps, had they not been separated so often, we would not have so many poems they wrote in exchange, we even have two that are each a hundred lines long written in the same rhyme from one to the other. This is not easy even in Chinese. Here is how Bai Juyi described their first years together after Yuan was sent away to Henan for something he said at court which was deemed too blunt. At the time, Yuan was twenty-eight and Bai, thirty-five. It was 806.

FOR YUAN ZHEN

Since becoming a minister of the court,
I have spent seven years in Chang'an.
And what have I gained but your friendship,
my dear Yuan. True friends are so hard to find.
There have been others, but like weeds on hilly slopes,
they disappear once rough winter winds begin to blow.
And high-ranking officers who call themselves friends

are unpredictable, their tempers are like ocean waves.
You are not like them because you never forget
promises you made, no matter how much time passed.
You are calm and reliable like water in an ancient well.
Like the autumn bamboo, you are honest and reliable.
We've become close friends, side by side every day,
from year end to year end, for three years now,
riding our horses under flowering summer trees,
laughing and sharing our wine even in the snow.
I welcome you at my door without ceremony,
not even bothering to don cap and gown.
In the spring wind, we sleep in till all hours of the day,
by autumn moonlight, we talk all through the night.
It's not because we sat for the exams at the same time,
not because we served at the same post these few years,
it is simply because we agree on what's important in life
and our agreement comes from the same place in our hearts.

贈元積

自我從宦遊，七年在長安。
所得唯元君，乃知定交難。
豈無山上苗，徑寸無歲寒。
豈無要津水，咫尺有波瀾。
之子異於是，久要誓不諼。
無波古井水，有節秋竹杆。
一為同心友，三及芳歲闌。
花下鞍馬遊，雪中杯酒歡。
衡門相逢迎，不具帶與冠。
春風日高睡，秋月夜深看。
不為同登科，不為同署官。
所合在方寸，心源無異端。

MY CHINA IN TANG POETRY

HAVING JUST SENT OFF BROTHER YUAN NINE

>Battered wutong leaves fall with rain,
>hibiscus petals fly off with the wind.
>The feel of early autumn is in the air,
>arousing a melancholy mood in me,
>and I have just said goodbye to you,
>how can I settle down and be content?
>Don't say I didn't come to say goodbye,
>my spirit was with you at Green Gate East.
>We don't have to have too many friends,
>so long as we share in our hearts' intent.
>My friend who knows my heart has left.
>All at once, Chang'an has become deserted.

別元九後詠所懷

零落桐葉雨，蕭條槿花風。
悠悠早秋意，生此幽閒中。
況與故人別，中懷正無悰。
勿云不相送，心到青門東。
相知豈在多，但問同不同。
同心一人去，坐覺長安空。

Bai's courtesy name is Le Tian 樂天, and that was how Yuan Zhen usually addressed him. Yuan Zhen's courtesy name is wEIZHI 微之, and that was what Bai called him most of the time. Other times, he addressed him as a brother. They wrote many poems to each other and of these, many are poems-in-response. The following are a few examples. The first pair is probably one of the early ones when Yuan was first sent away and the busy capital of Chang'an felt to Bai as if it had been emptied out. He was writing Yuan "secretly" because he was on duty at court as we are told in the third line.

SECRETLY WRITING YOU IN THE MIDDLE OF THE NIGHT
(Bai to Yuan)

Two full pages I have filled with the million strands in my heart,
hesitating to seal them in the envelop, reading them over and over
till the palace clock sounded the fifth night hour announcing dawn.
Like my desires, the lamp at my window has almost burnt to ashes.

禁中夜作書與元九

心緒萬端書兩紙，
欲封重讀意遲遲。
五聲宮漏初鳴後，
一點窗燈欲滅時。

ON RECEIVING LE TIAN'S LETTER (Yuan's response)

I walk in my front door with letter in hand and tears on my face, alarming my wife and making my daughter cry, wanting to know what has so upset me, having never seen this extraordinary sight: "The letter must be from Minister Bai," they said to each other.

MY CHINA IN TANG POETRY

得樂天書

遠信入門先有淚，
妻驚女哭問何如。
尋常不省曾如此，
應是江州司馬書。

The last day of the Third Month by the lunar calendar is later than March. It is called the End of Spring or the Last Day of Spring, another festival day; the Chinese calendar is full of days when family "ought to eat together." In the third line of the next poem, Yuan called his wife Meng Guang, one of the Four Great Ugly Women of China; obviously, he was referring to Meng's virtue, not her appearance! (She was one of the virtuous women in the poem Bai Juyi wrote for his new wife.)

AT THE REST STOP (Yuan)

It is the last day of the Third Month, the End of Spring.
Crestfallen, I gaze across the river from this scenic spot.
My Meng Guang expected me there on this last spring day,
but spring will have ended long before I can return to her.

望驛臺 (元稹)

可憐三月三旬足，
悵望江邊望驛臺。
料得孟光今日語，
不曾春盡不歸來。

We don't know if Yuan's wife wrote anything back in answer, but his friend, Bai, who was still in Chang'an, took it upon himself

FRIENDS AND LOVERS

to write twenty *jeju*s in response when he saw the poem. Here's one:

AT THE REST STOP

There's a weeping willow in front of your Jing An residence.
There's a carpet of fallen flowers at the rest stop where you are.
Spring comes to an end on the same day in two different places,
the one at home is thinking of the traveller, the traveller of home.

望驛臺 (白居易)

靖安宅裏當窗柳,
望驛臺前撲地花。
兩處春光同日盡,
居人思客客思家。

Then, it was Bai's turn to leave Chang'an:

ON HEARING THE NEWS OF LE TIAN BEING SENT TO JIANGZHOU (Yuan)

My dying lamp had gone out when the news came to me:
you have been banished to Nine Waters. Surrounded
by shadows, I sat up in a stupor, forgetting how ill I was.
A frosty breeze blew in raindrops through my cold window.

聞樂天授江州司馬

殘燈無焰影幢幢,
此夕聞君謫九江。
垂死病中驚坐起,
暗風吹雨入寒窗。

MY CHINA IN TANG POETRY

Around the same time, Bai wrote:

READING WEIZHI'S POEM ON MY TRIP (Bai to Yuan)

I brought scrolls of your poetry with me to read on my trip.
Daybreak had not arrived though the lamp was burning low.
My eyes were sore by the time I finished reading your poems.
In the dark I listened to the wind slapping waves on my boat.

舟中讀元九詩

把君詩卷燈前讀，
詩盡燈殘天未明。
眼痛滅燈猶暗坐，
逆風吹浪打船聲。

GRATEFUL TO LE TIAN FOR READING MY POEMS (Yuan's reply)

I heard you were moored on the west bank of the river,
reading my poems all through the night till daybreak.
I will stay up all night tonight here in lonely Tongzhou,
to listen to the cuckoos singing with the wind and the rain.

酬樂天舟泊夜讀微之詩

知君暗泊西江岸，
讀我閑詩欲到明。
今夜通州還不睡，
滿山風雨杜鵑聲。

FRIENDS AND LOVERS

Here is the spring picnic festival again. This time, Yuan was writing Bai:

REPLYING TO LETIAN'S MESSAGE OF THE THIRD DAY OF THE THIRD MONTH

We used to get drunk in front of these flowers on this very day.
Today, I am sitting before these flowers, killing time, being sick.
Alone, leaning by my broken window, feeling sorry for myself.
What a waste to spend such a beautiful spring day in this way.

酬樂天三月三日見寄

當年此日花前醉，
今日花前病裡銷。
獨倚破簾閒悵望，
可憐虛度好春朝。

SAYING GOODBYE ON SOUTH BANK (Bai to Yuan)

South of the riverbank, we said our sad goodbyes,
a misty west wind rose to proclaim autumn is here.
Every time you turn to look back, I hurt some more.
Take care, be safe, and don't look back at me again.

MY CHINA IN TANG POETRY

南浦別

南浦淒淒別，
西風裊裊秋。
一看腸一斷，
好去莫回頭。

In the next poem, Bai mentioned the Pen River, so we know that he was at Nine Waters; this is where he wrote the Pipa Song:

DREAMING OF YUAN NINE LAST NIGHT (Bai)

I rose early this morning to sit in the breeze, feeling wretched.
The Pen River is flowing toward you, but we are still cut off.
Were you thinking of me, or did something happen to you?
Why did you come to me in my dream at three in the morning?

夢元九

晨起臨風一惆悵，
通川溢水斷相聞。
不知憶我因何事，
昨夜三更夢見君。

GRATEFUL FOR LE TIAN'S DREAM OF ME
(Yuan's response)

Layers of mountains and rivers stand in the way of our letters,
thoughts of you thinking of me must have sent me to your dreams.
My spirit is low, and my body is weak from this dizzying illness.

Maybe that is why only people I don't care about enter my dreams.

酬樂天頻夢微之

山水萬重書斷絕，
念君憐我夢相聞。
我今因病魂顛倒，
唯夢閒人不夢君。

The next pair is famous for their Twilight Zone quality. In the first poem, Bai was visiting the Crooked Lake and the Buddhist Garden of Mercies with Yuan's brother and another friend, Brother Li Eleven. Yuan had already left for Liangzhou. In the second poem, written *at the same time* that Bai wrote his, Yuan had dreamt that he was there in Chang'an with them.

DRINKING WITH BROTHER LI ELEVEN, AND MISSING YUAN NINE (Bai, in 809)

The best time to dispel misery is when flowers are in bloom.
Drunk, I break a branch as payment for the wine you brought.
Suddenly, my friend sent to other side of the horizon, beckons.
Counting the days, he should be there at Liangzhou about now.

同李十一醉憶元九

花時同醉破春愁，
醉折花枝作酒籌。
忽憶故人天際去，
計程今日到梁州。

MY CHINA IN TANG POETRY

A LIANGZHOU DREAM (simultaneously, Yuan wrote)

I dreamt I was with you at Crooked Lake,
and then we visited the Garden of Mercies.
An attendant was waving at us to ride forward on our horses,
before I knew it, I was awake and found myself in Liangzhou.

梁州夢

夢君同繞曲江頭，
也向慈恩院院遊。
亭吏呼人排去馬，
忽驚身在古梁州。

The next two are from Yuan to Bai. Not clear when they were written, but they sound late, obviously they have parted more than once before. Also obvious is who Linglong might be; perhaps more obvious in the Chinese because her name means something like the tinkling of jewels. She was a singing-girl they both knew.

ANOTHER GIFT (Yuan)

Don't ask Linglong to sing my verses —
my verses are mostly songs of parting.
By dawn I'll be at the river. When the moon sets west
and the tide comes in, I would have headed out again.

FRIENDS AND LOVERS

重贈

休遣玲瓏唱我詩,
我詩多是別君詞。
明朝又向江頭別,
月落潮平是去時。

SENT TO LE TIAN (Yuan)

Doing nothing tonight, just sitting here thinking of you till daybreak.

Chasing old dreams, searching for old memories, feeling wounded.

Passing the exams together, meeting, wanting the same things in life,

we even received our first post together, and we didn't have beards then.

Twenty years have gone by as we make our way through this world.

Three thousand miles I have gone from Chang'an to this City of Lakes.

One assumes that there should still be a future in front of you and I,

is there someone we can seek out to ask which road we ought to take?

MY CHINA IN TANG POETRY

寄樂天

閒夜思君坐到明，
追尋往事倍傷情。
同登科後心相合，
初得官時髭未生。
二十年來諳世路，
三千里外老江城。
猶應更有前途在，
知向人間何處行。

Yuan died in 831. He was fifty-two. A few years later, Bai wrote the following poem where two people were mentioned: Wei was Yuan Zhen's little boy and Han was Yuan's brother-in-law. Zhangpu was where Bai was sent at the time.

A DREAM OF WEIZHI (Bai)

You came last night and took my hand, leading me out the door.
In the morning, my sobs soaked the washcloth laid on my pillow.
Zhangpu does me no good, three times I've fallen ill here so far.
Eight green Hanyang autumns have come and gone since
you were buried, now all that remain of you are your bones,
leaving me here among the living with a head full of snow.
Ah Wei and Han are both gone, one after the other, after you.
Did you hear? Or is news on earth denied you where you are?

FRIENDS AND LOVERS

夢微之

夜來攜手夢同遊,
晨起盈巾淚莫收。
漳浦老身三度病,
咸陽宿草八回秋。
君埋泉下泥銷骨,
我寄人間雪滿頭。
阿衛韓郎相次去,
夜台茫昧得知不?

5

Yuan Zhen and His Flowers

When Yuan Zhen met Bai Juyi after they both passed the Imperial Exam in 800, he was twenty-one and Bai was twenty-eight. At that time, Bai was still dreaming of marrying Xiang Ling, but Yuan Zhen had already had his first love affair. This is according to the story he wrote, *The Story of Cui Yingying*, which was based on his affair with his cousin when he was seventeen. In that story, the young man reneged on his promise to come back and marry his cousin who, even though she had "given herself" to him. Fortunately for her, she did eventually manage to get herself married to somebody else. In that story, he was the man who "extricated himself" from Cui Yingying and gave the impression that he suffered no remorse whatsoever. It is one of life's little jokes that this story will become the best known of Yuan Zhen's works and the reasons for its fame do not even have to do with the original story he told. It was made famous by the elaboration and artistry of a dramatist by the name of Wang Shifu 王實甫.

Yuan's story was to become the story on which the popular drama *Romance of the West Chamber, Xi Xiang Ji,* 西廂記 was based. The drama was written by Wang Shifu in the late 13th Century, and despite being based on Yuan's story, had quite a lot more substance. First, the heroine, Cui Yingying, was much more of a protagonist than a victim, and the story had a happy ending for the main characters. There were also many more poems in it and became so well-known that even characters from other novels quoted from it admiringly. Two of the best-known cases are the widely read 紅樓夢 *Dream of the Red Chamber* (mid- to late 18th Century) and 浮生六記 *Six Records of a Floating Life* (early to mid-19th Century). There were also retellings of this story in operas, movies, and television shows.

After Yuan passed the all-important *jinshi* exam, he was ready to look for a real wife, one who could promote his career, to put it bluntly. And this was when Wei Cong's father, a wealthy, distant relative of the imperial family, took notice of him. When Yuan Zhen found out that the youngest daughter of the Wei family was not yet betrothed, he started courting the father and successfully won the daughter's hand. They were married for seven years from 802 to 809. By all accounts they were happy, and Wei Cong was a resourceful and contented wife despite minor hardships, which were new to her as she came from a wealthy family, but she never complained. We know all this from Yuan Zhen's elegies mourning her after her death from illness. The most famous of these poems were the three "Mourning" poems but I had trouble translating them perhaps because I found it difficult to relate to them. For example, he opens with how she married beneath herself, the favorite daughter of a wealthy father, and then made do with vegetables, instead of meat, to stave off hunger. He then tells of how he begged her for money to buy wine when he ran out, and she sold her gold hairpin to satisfy him. He then expresses his regret that now that they were well-off because he was in a better position, she was dead. In the second stanza, he tells how he had followed her instructions and gave away her things, but couldn't bear to give away her sewing box, and how "extra kindly" he was treating her maids (presumably the ones she brought over when she married him) because of his fondness for his wife (one wonders how kind he was to the maids.) Then he talks about the paper money for the dead that he burned for her and utters the famous line "For poor, sickly couples, all things are worrying." In the third stanza, he feels sorry for himself and mourns. The poem ends with "I lie in bed with my eyes open all night long, /thinking how I can repay you for your kindness and wipe your frown away."

My account of his mourning may make you think that I am being facetious, and maybe I am, but this entire experience of finding out about Yuan Zhen's love life has helped me realize two things about myself as a reader/translator. First, I had always thought that I did not have to make friends or approve of the behavior of a poet or artist to appreciate his or her work. And to a certain degree I still think that is true. But, with Yuan Zhen, his careless abandonment of all these women (at least six that we know of, and I am not counting singing girls and maid servants) and his apparent pride or at least lack of concern for having done so, has colored my appreciation of his poetry. Secondly, it has reinforced the idea that, much as I love words and believe words have value, and to a certain degree I still do, words are just words, after all. Having said that, I have translated the following set of five, which are also among his best-known poems, although, for whatever reason, these five are not, like the above three, collected in the influential *Three Hundred Poems of the Tang Dynasty*. They are called "Thoughts after Separation" and were most likely written with his first wife in mind. Obviously, many little waterways were comparable or at least worthy of sailing on as "the open sea," even though he claimed in the fourth of these five poems, they were not. Here they are, the five poems of final separation, meaning death.

FRIENDS AND LOVERS

ON SEPARATION (Five Poems)

I loved looking at you as you sat at the mirror in the morning:
rumpled headdress, hairpins caught in delicate strands of silk,
and in no time, as the sun alights on your powdered cheeks,
you turned into a flower, newly awakened, just about to bloom.

Mountain spring water meanders gently along the city streets.
Ten thousand peach trees in bloom, pressing shadows on our loft.
Idly turning the pages of my Daoist scripts, too lazy to get up,
I watched you through the crystal blinds as you comb your hair.

Young women chase after the latest fashion
Recently it is myna birds dyed in the tender shades of wine.
You said it didn't matter that the fabric feels skimpy,
some irregularity in thickness makes it more attractive.

Having once sailed on the open sea, all bodies of water feel small to me.
Having seen Witch Mountain clouds, no other cloud deserves the name.
Were I to find myself among a million flowers, I would not care to look,
perhaps this is half the result of studying the Dao, and half because of you.

MY CHINA IN TANG POETRY

In the middle of spring among a hundred variety of flowers, I picked the pear blossom to present to the fairest of them all. Today, among the few trees standing by the river, I find myself in the company of leaves alone to pass the last days of spring.

離思五首

自愛殘妝曉鏡中，
環釵漫篸綠絲叢。
須臾日射胭脂頰，
一朵紅蘇旋欲融。

山泉散漫繞階流，
萬樹桃花映小樓。
閒讀道書慵未起，
水晶簾下看梳頭。

紅羅著壓逐時新，
吉了花紗嫩麴塵。
第一莫嫌材地弱，
些些紕縵最宜人。

曾經滄海難為水，
除卻巫山不是雲。
取次花叢懶回顧，
半緣修道半緣君。

尋常百種花齊發，
偏摘梨花與白人。
今日江頭兩三樹，
可憐和葉度殘春。

And yet, new blooms kept coming into the garden, or onto the flower market, that he hadn't expected to see before when he wrote that!

If he had written "On Separation" for his first wife, Wei Cong, nonetheless, he then went on to his next post and met the singer songwriter, Liu Caichun (in Chapter Five, Volume II of this series) sometime after 820. He lived with her for a while and then married, another wife from a well-off family, before he died at fifty-two. And then there was that other beauty that he "borrowed" from Bai Juyi, for a whole month, before he returned her to him, besides Xue Tao (also in Volume II, this one in Chapter Six) before he even met Wei Cong, not to mention his cousin whom he also abandoned in his youth. Who knows how many others there were?

CHYSANTHEMUMS

Chrysanthemums stud my yard as if I were in Tao's garden,
all along the hedges where the sun is slowly slanting down.
It's not that I am especially fond of chrysanthemums, but
when these flowers are done, there will be no other bloom.

菊花

秋叢繞舍似陶家，
遍繞籬邊日漸斜。
不是花中偏愛菊，
此花開盡更無花。

And this, too, was one of his better-known poems. What it is about is open to interpretation, since flowers meant women to the poet. Having dragged Tao Qian into the picture, though, was he saying he was not a recluse? All we can be sure of is that winter was on the horizon.

6

A Ghostly Talent: Li He 李賀

FALL IS COMING

Wind rustles through the wutong leaves, coming at my warrior-heart.
Lamp burns low as I listen to the shuttle of crickets anticipating winter.
Who will unfurl this bamboo scroll and read my writing? And how long
will it take for worms to make holes and turn my work to a heap of dust?
This miserable night and the thought of worms will surely pull my insides out.
But wait, the cold rain brings a ghostly figure, an ancient come to comfort me.
I hear voices singing from the grave, chanting Master Bao's rugged verse,[12]
a thousand years in the earth must have turned his aggrieved blood to jade.[13]

---

12 Master Bao is Bao Zhao 鮑照 who lived in the fifth century and is known for his *fu* rhapsodies. He was, like so many of these great poets, frustrated in his political ambitions and wrote a group of poems called "The Rugged Road", the verse Li He is referring to in this poem.
13 Zuangzi said of Chang Hong, another aggrieved virtuous man, that his blood will turn to green jade after three years in the ground.

MY CHINA IN TANG POETRY

秋來

桐風驚心壯士苦，
衰燈絡緯啼寒素。
誰看青簡一編書，
不遣花蟲粉空蠹。
思牽今夜腸應直，
雨冷香魂弔書客。
秋墳鬼唱鮑家詩，
恨血千年土中碧。

Li He lived a short twenty-seven years. He started writing poems when he was only seven, and by the time he was seventeen, his *fus* were compared to those of the contemporary stars of the genre. He was first noticed by Han Yu, a prominent poet and high-ranking official, who encouraged the young man to take the *jinshi* exam which would give him a chance for an appointment to a government post. (Han Yu, incidentally, was also one of the first scholar-poets to recognize the achievement of Du Fu's poetry posthumously.) At age twenty, Li He left for the capital, only to be disappointed because of something called a naming taboo; his father's name had a character that was a homonym of the name of the exam, *jin*. Thus, he was barred from taking the *jinshi* exam. Commentators have since surmised that this was not the reason, but one made up by those who were jealous of his talent. In any case, this resulted in his leaving the capital, returning home, and writing much angry poetry. Eventually, he was assigned a minor post because of his ancestry, but it did not last long. Soon, he contracted tuberculosis and died. Because of his unusual interest in the nether world, he was overlooked by Confucian scholars who tended to have been the arbiters of poetic merit for the longest time. He was not even included in the *Three Hundred Tang Poems*, compiled in 1763, and which aimed to tell us who were the important poets of the Tang dynasty. In more recent times, however, Li He had the distinct honor of being one of Mao Zedong's favorite Tang poets. He has also been given some attention by western readers since A.C. Graham included him in his popular but thin volume, *Poems of the Late T'ang* (Penguin: 1965; NYRB: 2008).

This next poem was written during one of his short stays in Chang'an. His rather lengthy preface to the poem provides the background. A couple of explanations are called for on its unusual title, "Singing with Bristly Shen on the Bili". A *bili*, 觱篥, is an ancient wood wind instrument, a sort of tribal trumpet constructed of reed and bamboo. Its sound is mournful and was sometimes used to frighten Chinese horses in battle. Shen had a beard, which is why they gave him the nickname "Bristly Shen," more literally it would be "Shen with a Beard". What I am calling a foot soldier is, in Chinese, "one who wears green on his head". This is because foot soldiers wrapped their head buns in a green cloth. In giving his friend's family background as "an honorable branch of the Li family with the privilege of offering sacrifice at the altar of Prince Jiangxia", Li is also telling us that he, too, was not a nobody. This poem could have been written when he was holding a minor post in Chang'an, which was what this status could bestow. Li Changji 李長吉 is Li He's courtesy name. The good-natured challenge described in the Preface would be something peers did, especially after a few drinks.

MY CHINA IN TANG POETRY

SINGING WITH BRISTLY SHEN ON THE BILI

Preface

Bristly Shen was a foot soldier under my friend, General Li, who was serving at the North Frontier. My friend, too, is from an honorable branch of the Li family with the privilege of offering sacrifice at the altar of Prince Jiangxia. Some years ago, he was sent away for a minor offense. He claims to be good at composing both five- and seven-character verses, even though he has yet to gain fame. In the fourth month of this year, he and I were boarding at the same hostel in Chang'an, Chongyi Lane, where our rooms faced each other. One night, he went and pawned some clothes for wine, and invited me and a few others over for a drink. When everyone had had a few and the party was going strong, he challenged me, saying, "Li Changji, you can handle seven-character verses quite well, I'll give you that, but you haven't proven yourself in the five-character line. Let me force your hand and ask to see how your skill compares to those of Tao Qian and Xie Lingyun. I'll bet you've yet miles to go before you catch up to them!" I thus asked Bristly Shen, who is an accomplished *bili* player, if I could compose a five-character *duanju*[14] lyric for him to play on the *bili*. When I completed the verse, the others demanded a performance. My friend was quite excited and stood up to call for his mistress[15] to come out and entertain us. I asked her what style of music she preferred, and she replied that she preferred the *ping nong* style.[16] Then, I adjusted the lyric to suit and requested Bristly Shen to accompany her on his *bili*.

---

14 *Duanju*, 断句, is similar to *jueju*, 绝句, but in stanzas.
15 Mistress is my interpretive translation of 花娘, *huaniang*, which means prostitute or singing girl, which men who could afford it travel with or temporarily "rent."
16 *Ping long*, 平弄, is a musical style which is slow and easy.

FRIENDS AND LOVERS

Flushed and inebriated, touched by your generosity,
we savoured the bili's haunting, plaintive tunes.
Stirred from sleep, headdress half undone, your mistress
appeared from behind the lotus screen to sing with the bili.
Who has made this heavenly instrument of
nine hollow stars carved into a bamboo body,
with the power to breathe life into flowers
and command clouds to scud about in the sky?
Tonight, I see before me youthful years passing,
years gone by and still to come, all for nothing.
Roused by torrents of emotions thus awakened,
startled, and frustrated, I can hardly sit still.
And you, my General, I see on a white horse,
with orchid sword raised high, strong and swift
as the macaque, catching fireflies in wild grass.

Li He and his host were both poor young scholars. These last lines are sad and funny. "Orchid sword" is just a fancy sword decorated with tassels. "Catching fireflies" is an allusion to a poor scholar in the Jin dynasty who was so poor he had no money for candles and had to catch fireflies and put them in a pouch for lighting to study into the night.

申鬍子觱篥歌　　並序

申鬍子。朔客之蒼頭也。朔客李氏。本亦世家子。得祀江夏王廟。當年踐履失序。遂奉官北郡。自稱學長調短調。久未知名。今年四月。吾與對舍於長安崇義里。遂將衣質酒。命予合飲。氣熱杯闌。因謂吾曰。李長吉。爾徒能長調。不能作五字歌詩。直強迴筆端。與陶謝詩勢相遠幾里。吾對後請撰申鬍子觱篥歌。以五字斷句。歌成。左右人合譟相唱。朔客大喜。擎觴起立。命花娘出幕。裴回拜客。吾問所宜。稱善平弄。於是以弊辭配聲。與予為壽。

MY CHINA IN TANG POETRY

顏熱感君酒，含嚼蘆中聲。
花娘篸綏妥，休睡芙蓉屏。
誰截太平管，列點排空星。
直貫開花風，天上驅雲行。
今夕歲華落，令人惜平生。
心事如波濤，中坐時時驚。
朔客騎白馬，劍弝懸蘭纓。
俊健如生猱，肯拾蓬中螢。

Li He was born in 790, the Year of the Horse, and died in 816 or 817. Chronologically, this makes him a mid-Tang poet, but we usually associate him with the late Tang because of his "decadence". Chinese people take their animal zodiacs very seriously; the fact that he was born in the Year of the Horse only makes his identification with the fine horses who were overlooked in the twenty-three horse poems to follow even more poignant.

HORSES

1

Along your dragon back is a pattern of golden coins.
Your canter is like silver hooves stepping on clouds.
No one has seen fit to dress you in satin saddle blankets,
or bothered to fashion an embellished gold whip to match.

FRIENDS AND LOVERS

2

In the bitter cold at year's end, you hunt for sweet grass roots.[17]
Capital city streets are covered in snow, like salt on the ground.
Not knowing if it's hard or soft, you must venture to take a bite.
Alas, what had looked like green grass was a thorny *bindi* plant.

3

The image of King Mu in his magnificent chariot rose before me,[18]
as he galloped up Jade Mountain with his team of eight fine steeds.
"Make Way for the King's Chariot!" His imperial ostler cried out,
as his favorite Flame-Red Beauty in the lead hurtled into the sky.

---

17 In order to survive the winter, grass stores sugar in its roots. The horse too must survive by looking for these grass roots, and not only is dead grass hidden under layers of snow, this poor horse bit into a *bindi* plant that is full of thorns.

18 King Mu was the fifth generation Zhou dynasty's king (1027-922 BCE). With him, we are in half-historic and half-mythological territory. He lived to a hundred and five. Here, he was riding to Kunlun Mountain, where the Queen Mother of the West lived. Many stories are born out of the Kunlun Mountain ranges, the longest mountain range in China. His chariot was pulled by eight fine steeds, who were "the best," and were chosen by a legendary ostler who was given a royal title. On this trip, King Mu met the Queen Mother of the West. They made love, and when he left, she asked that he come back. He never did, however, and therefore lost the possibility of attaining immortality.

MY CHINA IN TANG POETRY

4

This horse you see is not a common creature;[19]
born of an immortal star come down to earth.
Go ahead, knock on his bony frame and listen
for yourself for that extraordinary copper-sound.

5

He is born of the great desert where sand spreads like snow,
under the moon like a hooked halberd, on top of Mount Yan.
When will this horse have a golden bridle put on his head
and charge into autumn battle the way he was meant to do?

6

Starved for so long, his bony frame pokes into his parched skin.
Unattended, his coarse hair breaks the pretty pattern on his back.
His rich red mane is all dried up, his color is no longer radiant,
and the hair on his forehead is rubbed raw by a thick, jute rope.

---

19 A fine horse is supposed to make that "copper-sound" when you knock on its skeleton.

FRIENDS AND LOVERS

7

The Queen Mother of the West is in a drunken stupor.
The King of the East, her lover, is done with his meal.
If you should wish to head for the feast, My Lord,
who will you trust to head up your royal chariot?

8

None other than Lu Bu would Blood-Red Rabbit[20]
take on his back, but his master is no longer alive.
Dwarf horses there are, they will answer to anyone.
People say they will even let barbarians ride them!

9

Liu Shu An[21] had to leave in a hurry, he never returned,
now there is no one to tend to the king's dragon-horses.
The stable was blown over one freezing winter's night:
cold cracked the bones of these overlooked treasures.

---

20 Lu Bu, another Three Kingdoms hero, had a famous horse named Blood-Red Rabbit, who would not let anybody else ride him. The horse I have translated as dwarf horse is called "under-the-fruits horse" in the Chinese, meaning, it's so short that you can ride it under fruit trees. Li He is being condescending here to the "barbarians" who were attacking the Chinese border.
21 Another mythological character who was able to tend to and train dragons for the mythological King Shun.

MY CHINA IN TANG POETRY

10

He gave his Magic Steed to the ferryman to take away,[22]
but the horse is neighing against the wind, as if to say:
"King Xiang Yu, why have you cut your own throat today,
where can I find another brave and honorable master?"

11

Local horses are given to palace maids for entertainment.
They are dressed in fine silks with embroidered unicorns.
This beautiful horse pulls a salt cart under the noonday sun,
hungry and weak from fighting the oncoming wind and dust.

12

His ears have just grown out like cut bamboo stalks,
the peach blossom pattern has yet to appear on his coat,
but one day soon, when you need a fearless charger,
come back for him, and he'll be a leader in your battles.

13

Who was that aristocrat with the precious jade belt
and the reputation of a brave and just knight-errant?
He spent all that gold to buy the best horses there are,
all for a gift to unappreciative King Xiang of Chu.[23]

---

22 Legendary King Xiang Yu's horse was a black and white piebald.
23 He's calling King Xiang unappreciative because he killed himself and left his piebald.

FRIENDS AND LOVERS

14

A red silk scented shawl thrown over her saddle,
twirling dragons with glistening scales on her legs,
she looks back at me on that country lane going south
and tosses her head. Who says spring cannot be found?[24]

15

If Duke Huan had not taken his horse hunting,
he would never have known it could scare a tiger.[25]
If only they would take you for a run in the open fields
they will see how you can fly with the swiftest clouds.

16

When the King of Tang defeated the Lord of Sui,
Tang's First Emperor became master to Quan Mao.[26]
The full metal armor was never too heavy for him,
even with it on, he could outrun the windiest storm.

---

24 Running into a beautiful girl (or girl-horse in this case) is like finding Spring. When one has "a face-full of spring" it means one is in love.
25 Duke Huan of Qi (685-643 BCE) went hunting one day and came upon a tiger who, instead of attacking him, hid. He asked his courtier why and the answer was that his horse looked like the *bo,* a mythological beast that ate tigers and leopard, and therefore frightened the tiger.
26 Name of the horse the first emperor of Tang won when he won the battle against Sui and established the Tang dynasty.

MY CHINA IN TANG POETRY

17

Glistening knives are used to cut green wheat,
tender and fresh, finely cut for young horses.
Ponies with slender necks are popular as pets.
Stallions with long teeth are preferred for racing.

18

The man who could discern knew him instantly,[27]
pointing to the whorl between his chest and belly.
Now they are cutting back on his white grass feed,
will he ever be able to jump over the azure peaks?

19

At the Buddhist temple is a stunning white horse,
he had indeed come from India, bearing scriptures.
He has the appearance of kindness and mercy, but
he would never make it along the Zhangtai road.[28]

---

27 Bo Le of the Spring and Autumn Period is the man who could discern, meaning he knew his horses. White grass is a literal translation; apparently it is a kind of grass that horses prefer, but now its feed is being cut, so it might never be able to reach its potential.
28 Zhangtai is a busy road at the capital.

FRIENDS AND LOVERS

20

Riders in double-sashed swallow-tailed waistbands,[29]
each carrying a treasured fish-gut sword at the ready.
To equip them with ten-thousand-mile horses, one must
know how to pick fine creatures with mirrors in their eyes.

21

The magic horse, Soaring Gold, is here temporarily as a visitor,
the immortal will want him back when he leaves for Rainbow Tower.
Dress him in a bejeweled gold bridle until that time.
Don't send him away to the frontier in distant Gaozhou!

22

Sweat Blood arrived at the palace to join the Imperial entourage,[30]
jade ornaments and golden bits swaying to admiration and awe.
When people saw Shaojun by the seashore on the blue mule
did they understand that both mule and man were immortal?

---

29 The first two lines describe the warriors' elaborate clothing; the sword description is open to interpretation, fish-gut probably describing the curvy edged sword. The second two lines are essentially saying that appearance is not enough, you need the best horses to help you win. According to Bo Le (man in Poem 18), the best horses have eyes like bright mirrors that reflect a man's head and feet (i.e., the whole man) and shine with a purple brilliance.

30 Sweat Blood is the name of another good breed. Shaojun is Li Shaojun, a healer/magician of the Warrior King of Han. After he died, people saw him riding a blue mule by the water. When the emperor ordered his coffin exhumed, they found it empty. The blue mule, which had been pulling the emperor's carriage when it was alive, had become immortal and took Li to heaven. In other words, can people tell the difference without all that accoutrement.

MY CHINA IN TANG POETRY

23

The Warrior King wanted to live forever with immortals.
The gold he melted ended up in a column of purple smoke.
All they found in his stables were well-fed, meaty horses,
too heavy and too dumb to take him through the azure skies.

馬詩二十三首

其一

龍脊貼連錢,
銀蹄白踏煙。
無人織錦韂,
誰為鑄金鞭。

其二

臘月草根甜,
天街雪似鹽。
未知口硬軟,
先擬蒺藜銜。

其三

忽憶周天子,
驅車上玉山。
鳴驂辭鳳苑,
赤驥最承恩。

FRIENDS AND LOVERS

其四

此馬非凡馬,
房星本是星。
向前敲瘦骨,
猶自帶銅聲。

其五

大漠沙如雪,
燕山月似鈎。
何當金絡腦,
快走踏清秋。

其六

飢臥骨查牙,
粗毛刺破花。
鬣焦珠色落,
髮斷鋸長麻。

其七

西母酒將闌,
東王飯已干。
君王若燕去,
誰為拽車轅?

MY CHINA IN TANG POETRY

其八

赤兔無人用，
當須呂布騎。
吾聞果下馬，
羈策任蠻兒。

其九

騕褭去匆匆，
如今不豢龍。
夜來霜壓棧，
駿骨折西風。

其十

催榜渡烏江，
神騅泣向風。
君王今解劍，
何處逐英雄？

其十一

內馬賜宮人，
銀韉刺麒麟。
午時鹽坂上，
蹭蹬溘風塵。

FRIENDS AND LOVERS

其十二

批竹初攢耳,
桃花未上身。
他時須攪陣,
牽去借將軍。

其十三

寶玦誰家子,
長聞俠骨香。
堆金買駿骨,
將送楚襄王。

其十四

香幞赭羅新,
盤龍蹙蹬鱗。
回看南陌上,
誰道不逢春?

其十五

不從桓公獵,
何能伏虎威?
一朝溝隴出,
看取拂雲飛。

MY CHINA IN TANG POETRY

其十六

唐劍斬隋公,
拳毛屬太宗。
莫嫌金甲重,
且去捉飄風。

其十七

白鐵銼青禾,
砧間落細莎。
世人憐小頸,
金埒畏長牙。

其十八

伯樂向前看,
旋毛在腹間。
只今捋白草,
何日驀青山?

其十九

蕭寺馱經馬,
元從竺國來。
空知有善相,
不解走章台。

FRIENDS AND LOVERS

其二十

重圍如燕尾,
寶劍似魚腸。
欲求千里腳,
先採眼中光。

其二十一

暫系騰黃馬,
仙人上彩樓。
須鞭玉勒吏,
何事謫高州?

其二十二

漢血到王家,
隨鸞撼玉珂。
少君騎海上,
人見是青騾。

其二十三

武帝愛神仙,
燒金得紫煙。
廄中皆肉馬,
不解上青天。

    The Warrior King or the Warrior King of Han is a recurring figure in many poems of the Tang dynasty. As noted, he is often compared to the current monarch, either favorably or unfavorably. In the case of Li He's poetry he is, more often than not, used as an example of one who sought physical immortality but failed. In the next poem, Li He was stopping at his tombs in Maoling. To understand this poem, we have to bring in another character, who also appeared often in Tang poetry. She is the Queen Mother of the West.

The Queen Mother of the West is an important Daoist goddess, and she lives somewhere in the Kunlun Mountain ranges; Kunlun 崑崙 is a real, but remote, mountain range. The Kunlun messengers in the next poem are blue birds who belong to her. The birds bring messages of immortality, a sort of how-to script from her to whomever she chooses, and she usually only chooses emperors. She is the only Daoist deity who speaks directly to humankind and several ancient kings have petitioned her for elixirs, but each time they bungled her instructions in some way and failed to achieve it.

By the time human kings and emperors met her, she was depicted as a beautiful woman, but before mankind even existed and the Queen Mother of the West was still her demonic self, she appeared in the ancient 山海經 *Book of Mountains and Oceans*, a book of fairy tales, as a scary half-animal, half-human creature, with a tiger's teeth, a leopard's tail, and a wild mane. At that time, she ruled the West while the King ruled the East, and they were supposed to have been the first parents of all humanity, like Eve and Adam. Drinking dewdrops is supposed to give one immortal life—maybe it was included in the recipe she gave to the emperors she liked, and the Han emperor built large platters stuck on tall pillars to collect it. Qilin and Dragons are both mythological beasts that appear often in Chinese stories. Neither are supposed to die. Qiu-dragons have horns which may be curly; they are the ones you find wrapped around many palaces, and these days, restaurant pillars.

FRIENDS AND LOVERS

KUNLUN MESSENGERS

Kunlun messengers never came with news for you.
Tall trees surround your tomb now, shrouded in mist.
Your golden platter is filled to the brim with dewdrops,
but none of it can bring you back from the nether world.
The undying qilin's carved stone back is cracked with age.
Qiu-dragons wound round red pillars have broken claws.
Do the people's hearts have to be broken again and again?
This long night sees the bright moon shrink into the sky.

崑崙使者
崑崙使者無訊息，
茂陵煙樹生愁色。
金盤玉露自淋漓，
元氣茫茫收不得。
麒麟背上石文裂，
虬龍鱗下紅枝折。
何處偏傷萬國心，
中天夜久高明月。

Here, Li He is mocking the emperor, and his longing for the promise of immortality but also condemning this false belief or empty promise, which is a recurring theme in his poetry. One reason why Li He was so interested in immortality was because so many emperors were afraid of death, and no wonder, since there was so much intrigue and in-fighting among the ministers and eunuchs around the emperor that they were at risk of being killed, one way or another, all the time. As Li He was growing up, Emperor Shunzong, who ruled for less than a year, was rumored to have been killed by a plot hatched by eunuchs to put his son, Xianzong onto the throne, and through him, gain power

MY CHINA IN TANG POETRY

for themselves. In any case, Li He thought all the mumble-jumble of elixirs and drinking dew, and even melting gold and grinding jade to swallow, was a waste of the country's resources. On the other hand, he himself wanted immortality for his poems and, because of ill health, was often worried that his days were numbered.

The next poem begins as an angry lament over the passing of time, and ends up as an angry satire, making fools of all who wish for everlasting life. I translated the Ruo Tree 若樹 as the "If Tree" because the world *ruo* means "as if" or "if" as in "if x, then y". For example, if the Magic Dragon with the candle travels from east to west, then the earth is lit up during daylight hours. In killing the Magic Dragon, in the middle of the poem, Li He kills time and, thus, death. We need no longer hanker after the likes of Master Ren who was rumored to have ridden his donkey to immortality. Since 若 is a word in my grandmother's name, I have special affinity to it. Also, because the word means "as if", I think of it as a sort of amulet for translators and poets in general.

In the last couplet, he calls two emperors by their birth names. Liu Che is the Warrior King of Han and Ying Zheng, the First Emperor of China's Qin Empire. They were both eager to attain immortality and drank poisonous concoctions with bits of gold and jade powder. They were not aware these were poisonous at the time, of course, not even Li He knew; he only thought it was too extravagant. The Qin Emperor also built an elaborate mausoleum for himself in preparation for an afterlife.

The story associated with the Qin Emperor is that he changed sites many times when he was building his mausoleum, to prevent thieves and enemies from stealing his stuff and not to be able to get at his body after he is buried. So, when he died unexpectedly on a trip, his loyal guards hid him in a coffin made of catalpa wood under a pile of abalones to disguise the stench

FRIENDS AND LOVERS

of his corpse for the journey back to the capital. Catalpa wood is used for expensive coffins because of its rot-resistant quality. All this effort to preserve the body was somewhat contradictory. Nevertheless, that was what they did. We will see more of the Qin emperor in the Du Mu chapter coming up.

THE DAY IS BITTER AS IT IS SHORT

>Fly past, flying away, light of days!
>Have a drink on me before rushing by.
>I have no idea how far the dark sky reaches,
>how deep, the yellow earth,
>all I can see is the cold moon and the warm sun,
>burning away man's years.
>Eat bear and you grow fat,[31]
>Eat frog and you grow thin.
>Goddess of Changling, where are you?[32]
>Did the god Taiyi ever even exist?[33]
>On the eastern edge of the sky is the If Tree. [34]
>That is where the Magic Dragon with the candle lives.
>Let me chop off its legs,
>eat its flesh,
>so it can never travel again,
>and night shall never return.
>Then, the old need not die,

---

31 Bear paws and the fat on their back, only the rich can afford to eat. Frogs belong to the diet of the poorest of the poor. Anyone can catch them.
32 A young girl during Han times made goddess after her death. The Warrior Emperor of Han prayed to her for immortality on his deathbed according to the 史記 *Shih Ji* (*Book of History*).
33 Song Yu, poet (ca 290-223 BCE). This god is found in his "Gao Tang Fu," a fairy tale of Witch Mountain fame.
34 The ruo tree is supposed to be on the west side of heaven in the fairy tale. Plus, the dragon in the next line is supposed to be in the NW. Did Li He make a mistake? In any case, this dragon is supposed to carry a candle which lights up the world from dawn to dusk, just like the sun. That might be why Li He placed the Ruo Tree in the East?

and the young need not cry,
and there shall be no reason for drinking gold
and swallowing jade.
Who cares about Master Ren,
riding his donkey through the clouds?
Liu Che is just a pile of white bones under the Maoling Tomb.[35]
Ying Zheng in his catalpa coffin wasted all that abalone for cover.[36]

苦晝短

飛光飛光,
勸爾一杯酒。
吾不識青天高,
黃地厚。
唯見月寒日暖,
來煎人壽。
食熊則肥,
食蛙則瘦。
神君何在?
太一安有?
天東有若木,
下置銜燭龍。
吾將斬龍足,
嚼龍肉,
使之朝不得回,
夜不得伏。
自然老者不死,

---

35 Liu Che is the birth name of the Warrior King of Han. Maoling is the name of his tomb. According to *The Tales of the Warrior King*, 漢武帝內傳, the Queen Mother of the West said that despite his love of the Dao and pursuit of immortality all his life, he was just not immortal material.

36 Ying Zheng is the birth name of the First Emperor of China or Emperor of Qin. Abalone is valuable seafood. What a waste; I love abalone!

FRIENDS AND LOVERS

少者不哭。
何為服黃金、
吞白玉?
誰似任公子,
雲中騎碧驢?
劉徹茂陵多滯骨,
嬴政梓棺費鮑魚。

The next poem once again involves the Warrior King or Emperor Wu of Han, 漢武帝 (141-87 BCE). This time, he enters the picture with another emperor, Emperor Ming of Wei, 魏明帝 (226-239 CE). Wei's capital was in Luoyang, west of the Han capital in Chang'an (referred to in the poem as Wei City 渭城). I chose to translate it as Chang'an so as not to confuse the English reader. Just be aware, however, that the two *wei*s, Emperor Ming of *Wei*, where Wei 魏 is the name of the dynasty, and the city of Wei 渭, are two different words. Also, the orchid strewn road, Xianyang Road, was the road going out of Chang'an.

The bronze statue never made it to Wei. Along the way, the plate it was holding to collect dew fell and broke. Li He was mocking both emperors' wishful-thinking and extravagance. The line about heaven is used quite often by us even today. Instead of lifting the emperors to heaven by giving them eternal life, Li He brought the bronze statue to life! Interestingly, also, he called himself, "Prince" in the Prologue to this poem. Also, Prince Liu of Han in the first line refers to Han Emperor Wu.

MY CHINA IN TANG POETRY

THE EMPEROR'S IMMORTAL BRONZE STATUE'S FAREWELL TO HAN: A SONG

PROLOGUE
Emperor Ming of Wei, in the Eighth Month of the Year of the Green Dragon [237], ordered his palace guards to travel west to where the Emperor Wu of Han had constructed an immense statue of bronze, holding a giant platter, placed high on top of a metal column to catch the dew of immortality, and transport it back to Luoyang. He was hoping to place it in front of his own palace. The palace guards proceeded to dismantle the platter, and as they did so, tears fell from the statue's eyes. Thus, Tang dynasty's own Prince Li Changji [i.e., Li He] composed this song to commemorate the occasion.

> At Maoling tombs Prince Liu of Han lies, he who once mourned the autumn wind.
> Upon his death, his people heard the neighing of his phantom horse in the night.
> Autumn fragrance hung in the air drifting among stands of blossoming cassia trees.
> Everywhere in the thirty-six palaces, earth had burst into mounds of flowering moss.
> Emperor Ming's men have come a thousand miles to take Han's immortal statue west.
> Departing the Eastern Gate, the biting wind hit his eyes, drawing black bronze tears.
> No one came to see him off, only the moon of Han looked on in forlorn farewell.
> Still in service to the Lord of Han as he was torn away, strapped to the Wei carriage.
> Dying orchids on Xianyang Road silently wept, and waved as

they watched him go.
Had Heaven a heart, Heaven, too, would grow old.
With the immortal dew plate heavy on his shoulder, he watched Chang'an disappear
into the desolate moonlight, and before long even the sound of its waters faded away.

金銅仙人辭漢歌
魏明帝青龍元年八月，詔宮官牽車西取漢孝武捧露盤仙人，欲立致前殿。宮官既拆盤，仙人臨載，乃潸然淚下。唐諸王孫李長吉遂作《金銅仙人辭漢歌》

茂陵劉郎秋風客，夜聞馬嘶曉無跡。
畫欄桂樹懸秋香，三十六宮土花碧。
魏官牽車指千里，東關酸風射眸子。
空將漢月出宮門，憶君清淚如鉛水。
衰蘭送客咸陽道，天若有情天亦老。
攜盤獨出月荒涼，渭城已遠波聲小。

The third to last line: 天若有情天亦老, "Had Heaven a heart, Heaven, too, would grow old," is famously "lifted" by Mao Zedong for one of his own poems.

Li He's own emperor was Xianzong 憲宗 of the Tang dynasty, and like many emperors before and after him, he hankered after eternal life on earth and bought into the Daoist claim that this was possible. He summoned countless Daoist adepts to the palace to concoct recipes for elixirs. Li He wrote the following poem to mock his dream. The poem opens on the banks of the Silver River, which is the Chinese name for the Milky Way. Two stories to know for reading:

1. The Princess of Qin is Long Yu, Daughter of Duke Mu of Qin (221-206 BCE). She fell in love with the immortal

Xiaoshi who was a fantastic flute player and taught her how to play. She flew to heaven with him on a young blue phoenix after marrying him. The story is from the *Liexian Zhuan*, 列仙傳, *Tales of the Immortals*, the first Chinese book of fairy tales. Their story is often alluded to in Chinese poetry. Blue Island is where immortals live. Notice, her sun rises from the north, so it doesn't do what ours does, drive time. Nobody grows old in heaven.

2   Xi He, 羲和, is the god who rides the chariot that is, basically, our sun. Here, Li He is driving time and aging back into our consciousness. Thus, the poem ends back on earth and our daily revolutions, with land and sea changing places. Back on earth, dust and death defines our lives.

IMAGINING HEAVEN: A SONG

Revolving stars gather round the Silver River's shadowy banks,
as floating clouds burble in playful mimicry of watery sounds.
Evergreen cassias do not shed their flowers: the tinkling of jade
ornaments on palace maids is heard while they reap their scent.
Princess of Qin opens her northern blinds to watch the rising sun.
The blue phoenix waits on the pine by her window, forever young.
Playing on his goose-twilled flute, her Prince urges magic dragons
to tend to luscious fields of wild lingzhi and such life-giving herbs,

while pretty maidens in flimsy crystalline silk dresses drift among
Blue Island's swaying orchids in the flush of dawn, gathering spring.
Alas, here comes Xi He and his chariot of the blazing sun in the east,
and the ocean floor on earth is again exposed. Our life of flying dust!

天上謠

天河夜轉漂回星，銀浦流雲學水聲。
玉宮桂樹花未落，仙妾采香垂佩纓。
秦妃捲簾北窗曉，窗前植桐青鳳小。
王子吹笙鵝管長，呼龍耕煙種瑤草。
粉霞紅綬藕絲裙，青洲步拾蘭苕春。
東指羲和能走馬，海塵新生石山下。

Li He imagined heaven in many of his poems and they usually have to do with the theme of immortality in one way or another. Even though the above poem ends on an ominous note, the depiction of heaven is unusually positive if illusory.

The next poem, "A Dream Trip to the Land in the Sky," is a mix of fairy-tale information à la Li He. The rabbit and toad both live in the moon (see "The Story of Chang'e" in the Li Shangyin chapter, p. 188, which explains why the beautiful Lady in the Moon, Chang'e, is also a toad). The tinkling of jade means that a beautiful woman, immortal, or aristocrat is about to appear, because those are the people who wear jade. In this case, she/they is/are invisible, therefore, one or more immortals. Time goes by extremely slowly in heaven and as in many fairy tales all over the world, everyone who has been away in some paradisal place comes home to find that thousands of years have gone by. The "Nine States of Qin" is how the entire map of China was described in ancient times. "The Great Ocean" is the East China Sea. Li He seemed to be describing what the astronauts saw when they looked back to earth. He was also duplicating the Daoist sense of how small we are in the universe. Thus, so many Chinese paintings have little men standing in a vast landscape.

A DREAM TRIP TO THE LAND IN THE SKY

The old rabbit and a freezing toad sob over the gloominess of their days.
From cloud clad buildings, moonlight peers through half-opened doors.
Like a jewel wheel damp with dew, the moon appears, and the tinkling
of jade walks past with the drifting scent of cassias on this unfamiliar path.
Under the three immortal mountains a clear stream flows leading the eye
earthward where a thousand years have gone by swift as a galloping horse.
In the distance, the Nine States of Qin appear like nine dots of smoke.
Looking down, the Great Ocean is but a cup of water poured onto the earth.

FRIENDS AND LOVERS

夢天

老兔寒蟾泣天色，
雲樓半開壁斜白。
玉輪軋露溼團光，
鸞珮相逢桂香陌。
黃塵清水三山下，
更變千年如走馬。
遙望齊州九點煙，
一泓海水杯中瀉。

One might call "E Huang's Song" a travel poem. Li He was visiting Dongting Lake, a tourist spot. But this is Li He, so don't expect a sightseeing kind of poem. The Xiang goddess is the Goddess of the River Xiang. E Huang is the legendary virtuous King Yao's daughter. If she came back to earth, one could ask for her blessing. Here, however, she probably will never show. The White Stone Boy is a minor deity, and Li He may be identifying himself with the little god, giving up, after all this time, when nothing has come of his petition.

E HUANG'S SONG

At Lake Dongting, the moon casts its brilliance for a thousand miles.
Wild geese echo in the chilly wind, their crying bounces off the water.
Anemone rhizomes plucked and laid out on stones are dried out, dead,
while the Xiang goddess plays music to welcome E Huang's return.
Ancient mountain cassias have blown down their breathless

scent.

Tired of waiting, the dragoness shivers in the freezing watery light.

All you can see are schools of fish following the White Stone Boy,

as he carelessly tosses precious pearls into the vacant Dragon's Den.

帝子歌

洞庭明月一千里，
涼風雁啼天在水。
九節菖蒲石上死，
湘神彈琴迎帝子。
山頭老桂吹古香，
雌龍怨吟寒水光。
沙浦走魚白石郎，
閒取真珠擲龍堂。

Now for a harvest poem. The Harvest Dance is called "Second Year of Zhang He" because that was the year of a great harvest. Zhang He is the name of a Han emperor's year; they used to name the years of their reign, sometimes more than once. This was Emperor Zhang of Han (57- 88 CE), and the second year of Zhang He is 88 CE, which was the year he died, and that year, they experienced a great harvest. On the surface, the poem is utopian and ends with blessings for the emperor until the end of time. The fact that the emperor was already dead when the blessings were asked for, however, implies wishful thinking. In addition, the last line sounds like a prediction, that the Seven Stars will stop shining, and Chang'e, a mythological figure who should never die, dies. Why, one might ask, was this end of days image even introduced into an otherwise idyllic setting?

SECOND YEAR OF ZHANG HE HARVEST FESTIVAL
Wispy clouds cleared off
by the sweeping wind,
wheat like broomsticks upside down, millet like corn.
Everyone, men and women, wears many-collared robes.[37]
Tax-collectors have forgotten to harass them for rent.
Healthy buffaloes spring-ploughing dark fertile grounds,
and fields are irrigated along neatly divided plots.
They work the fields to benefit the likes of me,
and hire *qin* players to celebrate the occasion.
Flower-strewn valley like a white carpet, wild woods
filled with scent, inviting gods to come and enjoy
the feast set out by villagers. May they bless the Son of Heaven
with years, until the Seven Stars stop shining and Chang'e
   dies.

章和二年中

雲蕭索，
風拂拂，
麥芒如簪黍如粟。
關中父老百領襦，
關東吏人乏詬租。
健犢春耕土膏黑，
菖莆叢叢沿水脈。
殷勤為我下田鉏，
百錢攜賞絲桐客。
游春漫光塢花白，

---

37 Only the wealthy can afford many-collared robes. The Chinese reads "hundred collared."

MY CHINA IN TANG POETRY

野林散香神降席。
拜神得壽獻天子，
七星貫斷妲娥死。

This is how Li Shangyin began the short biography he wrote on Li He: "Li Chanji is a slightly built man with eyebrows that almost touch each other. His fingers are long and slender. He can recite poetry in a heartbreaking chant and write a fast script. Han Yu of Changni was the first to appreciate his talents . . . he did not pay attention to assigned topics, nor did he follow the prosodic rules to compose his poems. He was often seen riding a skinny donkey, with a boy in tow. The boy has on his back a worn and tattered quilted-cotton satchel. When Li was inspired by something he saw, he would quickly jot down a few lines on a piece of paper and toss it in the bag. His mother used to say, when they got home at night with a bagful of bits of paper with verses on them that she and a maid fished out of the satchel, "This child will spit out his heart [in verse] before he quits!" Then, she would light the lights and get him dinner. Li would then have the maid lay out the scraps from the satchel and he would arrange them into whole compositions and throw them back into the satchel. Unless he got very drunk or there was a funeral to attend, this would be his routine. His friends, such as Wang and Yang, would often come over to his house, pick the poems out and copy them. Then, they would take them away. Li would also ride his donkey to and from the capital and Luoyang all on his own. Sometimes he would write something while he was on the road and then carelessly toss it away, which was why Shen Ziming only had four scrolls of Li He's poetry collected in the end."

Death was never far from Li He's mind. Perhaps this was because of his own ill health, and because his father died when he was only eighteen. Here is how Li Shangyin, who heard the story from Li He's sister, described Li He on his deathbed. Apparently, "he saw a man in a crimson robe riding a red dragon descending from the bright sky coming towards him with a wooden plaque on which was written a summons in an ancient script. The summons was for him. Li could not read the script, but when it was read to him, he jumped out of his bed and kneeled, bowing his head to the floor, saying, "My mother is old and sick, I do not want to go." The man in the red robe smiled and said, 'Lord of Heaven has just completed his White Jade Tower and wants you to come and inscribe a poem for it. Life is happy in heaven, it's a good thing I came for you!' But Changji would not stop crying. Everyone who was there saw this. Changji sobbed so hard he could hardly catch his breath. Then everyone saw steam rising and coming out of the windows of his room. The steam rose in a column up into the sky, and they even heard a carriage and music faintly playing in the distance. Changji's mother tried to stop him from crying, and in the time it took to cook five bowls of rice, Changji breathed his last and finally died."

The ghosts Li He called up were not always about writing poetry or seeking immortality. We are not sure if he ever married, as there is no mention of a wife anywhere. Stories and rumors about his love life, however, existed. He wrote quite a number of poems for and about "singing girls". Here is one who has appeared more than once in his poems. Su Xiaoxiao 蘇小小 (circa 479-501) was a famous courtesan, singer, and poet, who has inspired many poems about her very short life. She is buried beside the famous West Lake. Her grave was destroyed in the Cultural Revolution and rebuilt in 2004.

MY CHINA IN TANG POETRY

AT SU XIAOXIAO'S GRAVE

Dewdrops on orchids,
like tears in your eyes,
there are no wispy branches here,
just wisps of mist to bind our hearts.
Grass makes a mat for sitting,
pine canopies offer shade,
breeze for your dress,
water your ornaments.
Your enamel carriage awaits,
ready to transport you at dusk,
with a chilly green lamplight
to accompany you where you go.
Visiting you at your Xiling tomb,
rain sends me chills in the wind.

蘇小小墓

幽蘭露，
如啼眼。
無物結同心，
煙花不堪剪。
草如茵，
松如蓋。
風為裳，
水為佩。
油壁車，
夕相待。
冷翠燭，
勞光彩。
西陵下，

FRIENDS AND LOVERS

風吹雨。

And here is another "love poem" for this ghostly lover. The Seventh Day of the Seventh Month by the lunar calendar is the Festival of the Weaver and the Cowherd, a story of forbidden and eternal love between a mortal and an immortal. After they were split apart, the Weaver is supposed to build a magpie bridge with real birds, and on it, once a year, she is allowed to be with her lover, the Cowherd. The Silver River is the Milky Way. Some say that Li He had a real lover in mind, but this sounds imaginary to me. This romance is the go-to story for Chinese poets when they feel sadly amorous or amorously sad, it seems.

EVENING OF THE SEVENTH NIGHT

In the depth of the Seventh Night, on the shores of the Silver River, they part
again, and she waits again, behind silk bed curtains, alone in a shroud of misery.
Like the Weaver's bridge-building magpies, wishful women thread their needles
and pray for talent, as fireflies blossom on the rooftops where clothes are aired.
Weaver and Cowherd come together: two stars like a broken mirror split in half.
Earthly lovers know their pain, pain like the half-moon's bright hook in the sky.
Where is my own Mistress Su Xiaoxiao and is she suffering, alone, just like me,
is she living out another endless, desolate autumn, another sad, miserable year?

MY CHINA IN TANG POETRY

七夕

別浦今朝暗,
羅帷午夜愁。
鵲辭穿線月,
花入曝衣樓。
天上分金鏡,
人間望玉鉤。
錢塘蘇小小,
更值一年秋。

Now for a pair of ancient lovers in Li He's not very romantic poem about his own frustrations, and not about love. Sima Xiangru 司馬相如 (179 - 117 BCE) was a musician, poet-scholar-patriot, and swordsman during the Western Han dynasty. He was a romantic figure and handsome. His courtesy name was Changqing 長卿. His greatest contribution to literature was the *fu* 賦, a form he developed, some say invented, and which became highly influential in later times. His political life was not nearly as unsuccessful as Li He's poems made it seem. Briefly, he left home in Shu (today's Sichuan) in his twenties for Chang'an and received a court appointment because he had enough money on him to give him the status of a gentleman. He was given the title of Mounted Military Attendant to Emperor Jin of Han. He was not thrilled with the position and moved to Liang to become a guest scholar at the court of Liu Wu, younger brother of Emperor Jing, Prince of Liang (the one in the poem). Here, he began composing the "*Fu* on Sir Vacuous," which eventually got him noticed by Emperor Wu of Han. The emperor and Sima Xiangru's interest in hunting coincided, and the poet wrote quite a few *fu*s for him and held good positions in his court, though they were not politically influential, and in Li He's assessment, somewhat insulting to his talents. Later, he was accused of taking bribes; whether this was true or not, he lost Emperor Wu's favor and Sima Xiangru had lost interest in court affairs by then anyway and retired to Maoling in 119 BCE. He died two years later.

In addition, there is the famous story of how he met his future wife and love of his life, Zhuo Wenjun, 卓文君. This was after the Prince of Liang died and he returned to Shu a relatively poor man. It was then that he met Wangji, the local magistrate who liked him and introduced him to Zhuo Wangsun, his future father-in-law, a wealthy iron manufacturer. Zhuo Wenjun was newly widowed at the time, and the two fell in love, but the father did not approve of their liaison, so they eloped. Their marriage was considered scandalous. During this period, they supported themselves by running a small wine shop. (Li He had this period of relative happy poverty in mind at the beginning of the first poem, even though he placed it at Maoling, where the emperor was to build his tomb, which came later). Then, the father came to his senses and recognized their marriage, after which they were no longer poor. In the end, when Emperor Wu heard that Sima was dying, he sent an official to collect his writings and preserve them. When the official arrived, the poet had died, but he left word with his wife to give the messenger a ritual scroll which he had written for the emperor and which was later used when Emperor Wu had his grand ceremony thanking the heavens and the earth, called *Feng Shan*, on Mount Tai. Feng Shan was an extravagant event, so it was a great honor that the emperor used Sima Xiangru's poem at the ceremony. Apparently only six ancient kings had ever held ceremonies of this kind.

In the second poem, which has next to nothing to do with the pair of lovers, Li He speaks of having "no elegant headscarf on [his] head," and gives a rather specific description of the color of his robe. This is because an elegant headscarf denotes status and,

MY CHINA IN TANG POETRY

as we have seen before, clothing in the Tang dynasty was color-coded. Also, in Chinese, as noted before in another context, the word "yellow" can describe either the color of the sun (therefore golden yellow) which only the king can wear, and the color of earth (therefore closer to brown) which is the color for serfs. The cork tree, Latin name, *Phellodendron amurense*, is a plant used for dyeing. It is bitter and the color of the dye is brownish. Since Li He is talking about his own death just a couple of lines earlier, he must surely have had the color of earth in mind.

SPEAKING MY MIND (two poems)

Changqing preferred the tranquility of Maoling
where weeping branches hung by the stone well.
He played the qin while watching Wenjun work
as the spring wind lifted wispy strands of her hair.
The Prince of Liang and the Warrior King of Han
used him ill and discarded him like a broken twig.
Yet he left the Warrior King a treasured ritual text,
gold dusted with mercury and read on Mount Tai.

Day and night I work on my scrolls, writing, writing.
One day, I am alarmed to see white hairs on my head.
Looking in the mirror, I laugh at myself, so young,
how can I reach South Mountain in time before I die?
No elegant headscarf on my head, and my robe
is dyed the color of earth with the cork tree bark.
Learn from fish swimming in the brook,
all they need is clear water to be content.

FRIENDS AND LOVERS

詠懷　二首

懷茂陵，
綠草垂石井。
彈琴看文君，
春風吹鬢影。
梁王與武帝，
棄之如斷梗。
惟留一簡書，
金泥泰山頂。

日夕著書罷，
驚霜落素絲。
鏡中聊自笑，
詎是南山期。
頭上無幅巾，
苦蘗已染衣。
不見清溪魚，
飲水得自宜。

Ending where we began, here's another angry poem by this talented ghost:

MY CHINA IN TANG POETRY

SINGING AT THE TOP OF MY LUNGS

South Wind flares its nostrils and flattens giant mountains.
God of the Universe rearranges massive waters on a whim.
The Queen Mother's peaches have ripened a thousand times,
and how often has Lord Peng and the Star of Sorcery died?[38]
Astride my green-copper-coin piebald, I take in the spring,
among tender willows, gently swaying in the silk-mist wind.
The pretty maid on the *zheng* is persuasive in her offer of wine,
saying, so long as blood flows in the body, who knows what awaits.
I need no wild bouts to be moved by "Ding Wu's Mournful Song," [39]
I know full well that true heroes will find no master here on earth.
I'll buy silk to sew a portrait in remembrance of Ping Yuanjun,[40]
and go before his tomb at Zhao with libation for his brave soul.
Water drops hitting hard, the jade toad with its mouth open chokes, and[41]
the pretty maid with Queen Wei's lush head of hair will see it combed thin.
Those dark brows, so shapely now, will also wither, and unlike green grass,

---

38 Lord Peng is Peng Zu 彭祖 an immortal and/or wizard and/or healer, some say he invented drums and could tell fortune. The Star of Sorcery is a shaman named Wuxian of the Shang dynasty, circa 1000 BCE.
39 Ding Wu's 丁旴 song about a 4th century warrior's tragedy.
40 Ping Yuanjun 平原君 defended the Kingdom of Zhao against Qin and held them off for three years.
41 The jade toad is a water clock, and Queen Wei in the next line is the Warrior King of Han's queen whose hair was thick and beautiful.

they won't grow again. So why waste my twenties toiling hard for nothing?

浩歌

南風吹山作平地，帝遣天吳移海水。
王母桃花千遍紅，彭祖巫咸幾回死？
青毛驄馬參差錢，嬌春楊柳含緗煙。
箏人勸我金屈卮，神血未凝身問誰？
不須浪飲丁都護，世上英雄本無主。
買絲繡作平原君，有酒唯澆趙州土。
漏催水咽玉蟾蜍，衛娘髮薄不勝梳。
羞見秋眉換新綠，二十男兒那刺促？

7

Du Mu 杜牧, A Sensual Man

The story was that Du Mu passed by a village called Wuzhou and saw a beautiful young girl who was only ten years old. He went to the parents and said that he would be back in ten years for her and gave them a large sum of money to have them promise that they would not marry her off to somebody else. It took him fourteen years to return, by which time the girl, now a woman of twenty-four, was married and a mother of two. When Du Mu complained, the mother of this woman said that her daughter had waited for twelve years before she finally married someone else. In other words, she was twenty-two when she stopped waiting, two years later than when Du Mu said he was coming back. They had not broken their promise, it was he who took too long to come back for her. Thus, he wrote the following poem.

SIGHING AFTER A FLOWER

> It was I who came too late looking for spring
> and not the flowers' fault for blooming early.
> A blustery wind has blown all the reds away,
> leaving branches of fruits in a shady canopy.

FRIENDS AND LOVERS

嘆花

自恨尋芳到已遲，
往年曾見未開時。
如今風擺花狼籍，
綠葉成陰子滿枝。

And, apparently, unlike Yuan Zhen, he never married anybody else. He was reputed as saying he would not marry anyone unless she was extraordinarily beautiful. I guess no one was beautiful enough in the end.

Du Mu came from an established family and led a relatively unscathed, although discontented life. He passed the *jinshi* exam at twenty-five, and held various minor posts during his lifetime, living in Hangzhou, Yangzhou, Luoyang, Xuanzhou, and several other places, but mostly in Chang'an where he was born. He died in 852, at only forty-nine. He is especially known for his *juejus*, particularly the seven-character ones, and of them, not surprisingly, the sensual poems about young girls and stunningly beautiful scenery. Besides those, he seemed particularly interested in historical events, and these provoked him to raise questions regarding destiny and will. His interest in history is not surprising; so many of our poets are also interested. In Du Mu's case, this interest was fostered by the fact that more than one of his positions had him working with historical documents. Let's begin with the indisputably famous of his poems (which might have surprised him). It was written at Chizhou in 846, so he was relatively "old."

MY CHINA IN TANG POETRY

QING MING

Qing Ming is a drizzly time of year. On the road,
people are falling over each other to find shelter.
"Where is the nearest drinking house?" I asked, and
the shepherd boy points to Almond Blossom Farm.

清明

清明時節雨紛紛，
路上行人欲斷魂。
借問酒家何處有？
牧童遙指杏花村。

This is Number 2 of the ten popular Tang poems picked by Hong Kong people in the survey in *Floating on Clouds*. Qing Ming is for visiting ancestors at burial grounds. The next two poems' popularity would not have surprised Du Mu.

Look up nutmeg buds, the first blooms bursting from the buds, to see why Du Mu is using this bud to describe his beauty. Also look at the fruits that will come later. Where I have "early spring," the Chinese reads "the second month," which means late February or early March. I wish she were a little older, but she's a young girl in a brothel in Tang Dynasty China.

PARTING GIFT (Two Poems)

Delicate and tender as a nutmeg in early spring,
she is just thirteen, the new year's first new bud.
Spring wind blows on Yangzhou's ten-mile-road,
lifting pearly blinds, and there's no one like her!

FRIENDS AND LOVERS

Always in love and yet I appear so loveless:
sitting before the bottle unable, to make a smile.
There's a heart in that candle, see how its tears
drip for us? Till dawn comes and I must go.

贈別　二首

娉娉嫋嫋十三餘，
豆蔻梢頭二月初。
春風十里揚州路，
捲上珠簾總不如。

多情卻似總無情，
唯覺樽前笑不成。
蠟燭有心還惜別，
替人垂淚到天明。

Here, I am compelled to repeat a comment I made on Li Bai's dalliance with some young "singing girls" when he himself was a young man.

"There are quite a few poems about young girls whose charms men find irresistible, and I do have reservations about translating them, because the girls were so young, and in many cases, they were "entertainers". Moreover, I have no intention to encourage the objectification of the "exotic Oriental" woman. Nonetheless, I find the best of these poems vivid and tender, and I remind myself that people died much younger, and they had to take on adult responsibilities much sooner. Fifteen and even younger was marriageable age at the time. Moreover, many of these scholar-poet-wanderers like Li Bai felt that they themselves were like these young women, forever on the asking or pleading end, trying to please, waiting for a morsel, forever looking in from the outside, on the fringes of society, looking into where they want to be in society. There is a famous couplet in Bai Juyi's "Pipa Song" that runs: "Castaways, we drift together and part again, / I know you well without knowing you at all," that expresses this sentiment very well."

In Du Mu's case, I find it harder to justify, because he was, it would seem, objectifying these beautiful young things. They are, to him, it seems, "thing[s] of beauty," like Grecian Urns. Or, you might say, they are like beautiful scenery! The saving grace is that his feelings were true and tender. As discussed in the Preamble, critics have often defended him by describing his appreciation of beauty as one of "pure pleasure unsullied by lust" 樂而不淫. His appreciation of the beauty of young girls seems to come from the same place as his appreciation of the beauties in nature such as in the following poems.

UP ON THE MOUNTAIN, GAZING FROM MY CARRIAGE

> Climbing up the cold stones of the steep mountain slope,
> looking out through to where clouds descend on houses,
> across from where the sun is setting on the maple forest,
> red leaves are glowing livelier than flowers in early spring.

山行

> 遠上寒山石徑斜，
> 白雲生處有人家。
> 停車坐愛楓林晚，
> 霜葉紅於二月花。

Southern Dynasties in the next poem refers to the culturally rich but politically weak period from 420 to 589.

FRIENDS AND LOVERS

JIANGNAN SPRING

Ten thousand miles of warblers' songs, shades of greens and reds,
watery villages on hilly slopes, winery banners waving in the wind,
four hundred eighty temples and shrines left from Southern Dynasties,
and just as many pavilions and terraces are caught in the misty rain.

江南春

千里鶯啼綠映紅，
水村山郭酒旗風。
南朝四百八十寺，
多少樓台煙雨中。

CREPE MYRTLE

In the morning dew of autumn, you have just awakened,
what matters if you were not the new year's first bloom?
Pear and plum blossoms have silently come and gone,
yet you are still here, laughing with me under the sun.

紫薇花

曉迎秋露一枝新，
不佔園中最上春。
桃李無言又何在，
向風偏笑艷陽人。

MY CHINA IN TANG POETRY

MOORED AT QIN RIVER

The gauzy moonlight cast a misty net over this cold river, drawing me towards the brightly lit area of pleasure seekers. Unaware of the bitterness of a nation's fall, working girls across the river are still singing "Flowers in the Backyard".

See p.28 for mention of this song.

泊秦淮

煙籠寒水月籠沙，
夜泊秦淮近酒家。
商女不知亡國恨，
隔江猶唱後庭花。

Just as knowing what a nutmeg bud looks like helps in the appreciation of Du Mu's "Parting Gifts," it would help to know what willows, lotus and wutong leaves look like and why they appear so often in Chinese poems. Most of us in the West know willows, even banks of them, but are you aware that lotus leaves can grow very tall? So tall that one could row boats underneath their gigantic parasol-like leaves? Or that wutong trees have green trunks and also have pretty large leaves? The closest I can come to describing wutong leaves, is that they look like large fig leaves, growing very densely, almost like a head of hair growing on the trees. Knowing their flora and fauna is very important to Chinese scholars, not only because Confucius in the North says so, but because they are also found in the oldest poetry of the South. As I claimed elsewhere, knowing one's plants has much to do with good governance, according to Confucius.

FRIENDS AND LOVERS

POSTED AT QI AN PROVINCE
(Two impromptu poems)

On the little bridge across the brook, I watch the sun set
low among the shadowy willows over by the misty bank.
Bright green lotus leaves grown tall, leaning on each other,
till a sudden gust turns their heads against the west wind.

Fall sounds stir the homesick heart wherever it finds itself:
in faraway Cloud Dream Swamps caught in torrential rain,
or outside my front steps under raindrops on wutong leaves.
Why am I so moved by their mournful sobbing in the wind?

齊安郡中偶題二首

兩竿落日溪橋上，
半縷輕煙柳影中。
多少綠荷相倚恨，
一時回首背西風。

秋聲無不擾離心，
夢澤蒹葭楚雨深。
自滴階前大梧葉，
幹君何事動哀吟？

MY CHINA IN TANG POETRY

Turning to his poems with historical interests, I find that even they often have something to do with women or passion. Having said that, the first poem, "Traversing Black Horse Mountain," will only hint at those topics. It has to do with unpredictability, which seems to be Du Mu's view of history and life's ironies. I am dating this poem 826, which makes Du Mu twenty-three, partly because it sounds a bit immature and partly because in that same year, he had written a long satire on the same subject as "Traversing Black Horse Mountain" to warn the presiding administration about their extravagance and neglect of people's welfare, using the destruction of the Qin Empire as example of how misgovernment and cruelty brought an end to it. We call the man who formed that first empire Qin Shi Huang, meaning, the First Emperor of Qin. He united, that is, conquered, six states plus his own, to form the first empire and it lasted for only fifteen years (221-206 BCE).

In 1974, The First Emperor's mausoleum with the terracotta warriors was discovered by archaeologists in Xi'an, which is the old Chang'an, but in 826, they did not know that the mausoleum still existed. In 826, they thought the First Emperor's extravagant tomb had been burned in an accident involving a shepherd boy who went looking for his sheep with a torch (see last two lines in the poem). Even though the First Emperor's many accomplishments in the realms of law and government, irrigation and engineering, and standardization of the written language, were well-known, what is often emphasized is his burning of books he did not like, such as the Confucian texts, and his burying alive of people he did not agree with, e.g., Confucian scholars. Indeed, many builders and soldiers were killed in the erection of the Great Wall and his Mausoleum; the Great Wall was begun but not nearly finished by him. In this poem by Du Mu, he was emphasizing the emperor's extravagance and cruelty to reflect on the present Tang Emperor, Jingzong, who was only fifteen when he ascended the throne and would soon be assassinated by eunuchs when he reached his seventeenth birthday. Since the emperor was only a teenager at this time, it should not surprise us that he was only interested in partying and not ruling. In any case, both he and his brother who was to succeed him were really emperors in name only.

The first half of the poem tells of the anecdotal incident of Liu Bang and Xiang Yu having been among the onlookers in the countryside when the Qin Emperor went looking for one of the lost tripods of the Zhou dynasty. These tripods were "sacred" because they symbolized the previous dynastic rule's power and legitimacy, and for the Qin Emperor to have them would support his own claim to legitimacy. Obviously, he was a very insecure ruler. He apparently sent a thousand divers looking for it in the Si River where it was supposed to have been lost, to no avail. "Liu and Xiang" were just poor peasants at this time, but eventually, Liu Bang would become the founding emperor of Han, and Xiang Yu would be a great general who revolted against Qin's young emperor when the first one died, and the two of them, Liu and Xiang, would be fighting each other eventually to gain control of the whole kingdom.

Black Horse Mountain is my translation of Lishan 驪山, a historically significant scenic area in Xi'an. (As I explained before, 驪 *li*, means a pure black horse, made up of the radical for horse and the word for beautiful.) This is where the Tang Emperor Xuanzong built the famous resort for his lovely consort Yang Guifei. In this poem, Du Mu is the tourist, and he was referring to the Qin Emperor's Tomb which was supposed to have been in the underground of Lishan as well. The place must have good feng sui for all these emperors to have chosen to build on it or in it. Even though he only started building the Great Wall, many had died building it, and the Chinese imagination pretty much identifies him with it. It was Mencius, Mengzi 孟子 (372-289 BCE) who said that "the one who brings together the Four Seas [i.e., unites the country] is called the Son of Heaven, but should the people under heaven rebel against him, he will be called "a man alone" 獨夫. This is what Du Mu was alluding to in the opening of the second verse here. Since Mencius was Confucius's disciple, Du Mu would have been thinking of the First Emperor's burying of the Confucian scholars as well by this allusion.

TRAVERSING BLACK HORSE MOUNTAIN

When Emperor Qin went searching for the Zhou tripod,
Liu and Xiang were stretching their necks to catch a glimpse.
Such hard work, uniting seven kingdoms to make them one,
only to have your throne swallowed up by two commoners.
It's not the foolishness of the people that brought you down,
it is that thousand-mile wall that made you "a man alone."
And you and your treasures underground, burnt to a cinder
by a shepherd boy, even before they could rot in the ground.

過驪山作

始皇東遊出周鼎，
劉項縱觀皆引頸。
削平天下實辛勤，
卻為道傍窮百姓。
黔首不愚爾益愚，
千里函關囚獨夫。
牧童火入九泉底，
燒作灰時猶未枯。

FRIENDS AND LOVERS

So, what happened to Liu Bang 劉邦 and Xiang Yu 項羽? That story has many twists and turns to it as well, and numerous instances of heroism and betrayal, and historians are still debating the characters of these men. Suffice it to say here that in the end, Liu Bang won and became the first emperor of the Han dynasty (202 BCE-220 CE). On the other hand, Xiang Yu has won many sympathizers throughout history, despite losing the final battle and slitting his own throat. Li Qingzhao, an important woman poet of the late Song dynasty, for example, wrote a *jueju* claiming Xiang Yu to be her hero. Here's her poem, "*Jueju* written on a Summer's Day" at the spot where Xiang Yu was supposed to have killed himself, refusing to cross the river to go back east. (The opening chapter of my Song poetry series is devoted to her story.)

> A superman in your own lifetime,
> you are a hero now among ghosts.
> Today, in remembrance of Xiang Yu,
> I will not cross this river to the east.

> 生當作人傑，
> 死亦為鬼雄。
> 至今思項羽，
> 不肯過江東。

Du Mu, who thought Xiang Yu should have crossed the river, came to a different conclusion.

Briefly, Xiang Yu was born in 232 BCE and died in 202 BCE. He was a giant of a man and very strong. To cut a long story short, he led a rebellion against the cruel emperor of Qin and became a warlord, and indeed "knighted" Liu Bang and made him a nobleman, though Liu was older than himself. Then, Liu

MY CHINA IN TANG POETRY

Bang rose up against him and, after many battles, Xiang Yu lost. When he arrived at the Wu River's edge and the enemy soldiers were at his heels, he recited a poem that, to this day, many still quote, especially when they feel hopeless. He then cut his own throat. The poem is short but compelling and my translation is not up to the task, but I shall give it to you anyway, just so you have an inkling. It is called 垓下歌, Song of Gaixia, the place where this battle was fought:

> I can pull up mountains with my bare hands — ai — that's the life force in me.
> Yet the times are against me — ai — and my horse is tired.
> My horse is tired — ai — what can I do?
> Lady Yu — ai — Lady Yu — ai — tell me what I can do!

垓下歌

力拔山兮氣蓋世，
時不利兮騅不逝。
騅不逝兮可奈何，
虞兮虞兮奈若何！

There's that pause particle we saw in Li Bai's two poems, "Wind Song in the Fall" and "Torn Away" (Volume I, p. 82). It is very powerful to the Chinese ear. As the story goes, Lady Yu, his one true love, had already cut her own throat earlier. Now for Du Mu, at that same spot:

FRIENDS AND LOVERS

WRITTEN AT CROW RIVER KIOSK

Winning and losing on the battlefield is unpredictable,
what makes a man is his ability to bear insults and pain.
Strong warriors east of the river were waiting for your return,
had you not quit, who knows, you could've turned the tide!

題烏江亭

勝敗兵家事不期，
包羞忍恥是男兒。
江東子弟多才俊，
捲土重來未可知。

Du Mu also wished for his success and was frustrated that he didn't cross the river to go home and survive to fight another day. In the last line, 捲土重來 literally, "roll up the earth [like a rug] and come again," meaning survive to fight another day or make a comeback, has become another set phrase in everyday usage. I had to give up the image in my translation.

Backstory to Red Cliff

The next poem and the story that goes with it is one that involves another Liu. Liu Bei came twelve generations after Liu Bang, one at the beginning of the Han Dynasty and the other at the end. There is some speculation that the latter Liu may be the first Liu's descendant, but there is no certainty. Red Cliff is in today's Hubei, and the site of a famous battle by that name: 赤壁, Chibi, which means Red Cliff. This battle was fought in 208 among the leaders of what would become the Three Kingdoms. If you go there today, you will see the characters 赤 *Chi* and 壁 *Bi* painted in red on the cliff that some historians claim was where the Battle

MY CHINA IN TANG POETRY

of Chibi was fought. It was this battle that enabled Liu Bei and Sun Quan to establish themselves in the south against Cao Cao in the north. Thus, the Three Kingdoms were formed. As told in *Romance of the Three Kingdoms*, it was the plan of Zhuge Liang, Liu Bei's military strategist's, in which he used the wind coming from the east to spread fire over to Cao Cao's warships that won them this victory. Master Zhou, which I translated as Zhou Yu (his whole name), was Sun Quan's military general and he was the one instructed to use Zhuge Liang's plan, but Du Mu chose to give credit to him rather than Zhuge Liang. Thus, in the third line in Du Mu's poem where he asked the hypothetical question of what if the east wind hadn't come, we have him calling it "Zhou Yu's plan". The Qiao sisters in the fourth line were two beautiful sisters. One was married to Sun Ce, Sun Quan's brother whom he succeeded, and one to his military general, Zhou Yu. The Brass Bird Tower was built by Cao Cao and a sort of pleasure dome. As the story goes, Cao Cao also had his eye on the Qiao sisters at one time. I capitalized the East Wind in my translation as this was almost sacred, like a godsend called up, as I understand it, by Zhuge Liang.

There is a familiar expression that came from this part of the story which goes 萬事俱備, 只欠東風 "All things are readied, the only thing lacking is the East Wind," attributed to Zhuge Liang as reimagined by Luo Guanzhong 羅貫中 in the Ming Dynasty novel 三國演義 *Romance of the Three Kingdoms*, which post-dates Du Mu, although the history on which the novel is based was, of course, familiar to him. All this to say, modern readers of this stretch of history will inevitably be looking at it through the influential novel's telescope and want to know why Zhuge Liang is not given credit for bringing on the East Wind in Du Mu's picture. My guess is that Du Mu's attention, as is often the case, landed on the beautiful Qiao sisters and the romance they bring to the story, since Zhou Yu was married to one of them. Besides, he never read the novel!

Here is the little poem I am talking about:

RED CLIFF

I came upon a rusted piece of halberd half-buried in the sand,
cleaned it and thought it must be from that old battle long ago.
And what if the East Wind had not complied with Zhou Yu's plan,
would the Qiao sisters have been locked in the Brass Bird Tower?

赤壁

折戟沉沙鐵未銷，
自將磨洗認前朝。
東風不與周郎便，
銅雀春深鎖二喬。

The next three poems take us back to Black Horse Mountain and the destructive beauty, the Imperial Consort Yang Guifei. Black Horse Mountain is where the hot spring resort that Emperor Xuanzhong built for her enjoyment called Hua Qing Gong 華清宮, translated here as "The Pool of Blossoms Palace". Her story is told in detail in *Superstars*. Brief background information for the three poems here:

Poem 1) The lychee was the Consort's favorite fruit. It is one of the stories that illustrate Xuanzong's fondness for her and his extravagant habits. Apparently, he would send swift riders to fetch lychees for her once they ripen, because the season does not last long and they need to be eaten fresh.

Poem 2) Xin Feng is a town near Black Horse. Yu Yang is where An Lushan's hide-out used to be. (See "War drums from Yu Yang" in "Curse of Passion" on p. 50 above.) The horsemen were sent to investigate and see if An really had rebellious intentions. An bribed them heavily to come back with a false report, and so the Emperor partied till Chang'an fell. "Song of the Rainbow Skirts" was allegedly composed by the Emperor and Yang Guifei. The royal entourage stayed on Black Horse till An Lushan captured Chang'an and they had to run to Shu in the south.

Poem 3) Apparently An Lushan was very fat, so much so his belly hung over his knees, but he was a good comic dancer and often performed for the Emperor and his Consort who enjoyed his antics. The music he danced to was tribal; that was why Du Mu described it as "bewildering," and it confused the existing court music.

PASSING BY THE POOL OF BLOSSOMS PALACE
(three poems)
1

Looking back from Chang'an, carpets of embroidered flowers covered the mountainside, and a thousand doors opened one by one.
A storm of dust arrived with the horses, brought a smile to the Consort's face.
Who would've guessed it was just lychees being delivered by the swift riders.

2

Xin Feng's green trees are covered in a shower of yellow dust,
raised by the horsemen returning from their Yu Yang inquiry.
"Song of the Rainbow Skirts" penetrated Black Horse's peaks.
They danced till the capital was besieged and they had to run.

3

Wanton songs and dances possessed our country drunk on peace,
palaces reached into the night sky, lit up by the brilliant moon.
Bewildering rhythms accompany Lushan's swaying and twirling.
When the wind blew this way, people heard royal fits of laughter.

過華清宮 （三首）

長安回望繡成堆，
山頂千門次第開。
一騎紅塵妃子笑，
無人知是荔枝來。

新豐綠樹起黃埃，
數騎漁陽探使回。
霓裳一曲千峰上，
舞破中原始下來。

萬國笙歌醉太平，
倚天樓殿月分明。
雲中亂拍祿山舞，
風過重巒下笑聲。

MY CHINA IN TANG POETRY

"Taking to Mount Ci on the Ninth": A Reading

The following poem seems simple until we recognize the allusions seamlessly woven into its let's-make-merry lines. This short piece was written in 844, on his friend Zhang Hu's visit. Zhang had retreated to Jiangsu, having been denounced by our old friend Yuan Zhen. This trip to Cizhou to visit his good friend Du Mu was in sympathy to Du Mu's own political troubles. They were both going through a rough patch in their careers. The occasion, ostensibly, is the Chong Yang festival, when people take a break from everyday life to go up a mountain, or some high place, for a picnic. Originally, it was to avoid disaster. So, in the title and the opening lines, we are given the setting (Mount Qi), the season (wild geese, therefore fall), the occasion (the Ninth), the friend (Zhang, though not directly named), the wine and the picnic. The first allusion is to Zhuangzi, who said, basically, life is hard, what with sickness and deaths and other interruptions to living, people only get to laugh, on average, four or five times a month. Thus, Du Mu says, we need to take every opportunity to have fun.

Having brought Zhuangzi into the poem, we are to recall his attitude towards life, that is, the Daoist one of "letting be". Zhuangzi famously beat his drums at the death of his wife (open to interpretation). Then we have the chrysanthemums, which bring Tao Qian to mind. Du's friend Zhang is obviously also an admirer, as he himself has gone into "hiding". (Remember Tao Qian's name? "Hiding" means going into reclusion. See Preamble to Volume II).

Finally, Master Jing is a person from the Spring and Autumn period (770 BCE-476 BCE) who wept at the sight of Bull Mountain because of his nation's fall. So, the mention of him is Du Mu's way of saying, we are worried about the state of our nation, but since there is nothing we can do to change things, we are not

FRIENDS AND LOVERS

going to weep. This is the time to get drunk and act like wild men with chrysanthemums in our hair!

MARKING THE NINTH ON MOUNT QI

Wild geese flying across the water's surface tell me fall is here.
I bring wine and invite my friend up this jewel-green mountain.
Why miss this opportunity for an outing and a few laughs besides?
Chrysanthemums in full bloom should be worn all over our heads.
Let's get plastered and truly celebrate this Double Ninth.
Why fret over useless regrets and the dying of the light?
Ancient times, modern days, it's ever been the same.
What use is Master Jing's sobbing at Bull Mountain?

九日齊山登高

江涵秋影雁初飛，
與客攜壺上翠微。
塵世難逢開口笑，
菊花須插滿頭歸。
但將酩酊酬佳節，
不用登臨恨落暉。
古往今來只如此，
牛山何必獨沾衣。

And here are three more beautiful women. In the first poem, we find the passionate beauty Green Pearl who jumped off the tower to show her loyalty for the man who loved her. Her story is told in Volume I, Chapter Five.

MY CHINA IN TANG POETRY

GARDEN OF GOLDEN VALLEY

After the glitz and glamor dispersed, dust and ashes remain.
Flowing water, green grass in spring, have no feelings for you.
East wind in the evening, the cry of birds when flowers fall,
call to mind that passionate beauty who stepped off the tower.

金谷園

繁華事散逐香塵，
流水無情草自春。
日暮東風怨啼鳥，
落花猶似墮樓人。

In this second poem, Du Mu conjures up a young palace maid, idly flapping fireflies and gazing at the night sky. And here again are the Weaver and Cowherd lovers.

AUTUMN EVENING

In silvery candlelight the picture screen appears cold.
You flap at flitting fireflies with your gauzy silk fan.
Palace steps shimmer in the cool evening like river water,
as you lean back admiring the Weaver and Cowherd stars.

秋夕

銀燭秋光冷畫屏，
輕羅小扇撲流螢。
天階夜色涼如水，
臥看牽牛織女星。

FRIENDS AND LOVERS

For the next poem, readers are unclear whether there were twenty-four bridges, or one bridge called Twenty-Four Bridge. Also, there is one suggestion that the twenty-four refers to the number of ladies on the bridge playing the flute as opposed to the bridge. The visual of twenty-four bridges appeals to me, so I have made that choice. Also, since the Chinese says, "Beautiful one, where are you teaching [or being taught] how to play the flute," and since "beautiful one" can either be referring to the scholar/magistrate or to a beautiful lady, I have chosen to include them both and carry on the somewhat suggestive idea of them playing the flute together, whether it is him teaching her or her playing for him.

SENT TO MAGISTRATE HAN CHOU AT YANGZHOU

Hazy hills and rivers reaching far away into the distance,
it's autumn's end here, but down south, grass has yet to wither.
On a bright moonlit night like this on Twenty-Four Bridges,
what pretty lady might you be playing the flute with tonight?

寄揚州韓綽判官

青山隱隱水迢迢，
秋盡江南草未凋。
二十四橋明月夜，
玉人何處教吹簫。

We don't remember him as "a heartless cad", as he calls himself in this next poem but, as Bai Juyi said of Emperor Xuanzong, Du Mu was surely "a sensual man". Thank goodness he didn't have a kingdom to lose nor was this lover of beauty a cruel and heartless bully in power! I left out 青樓 in my translation, which, by Tang times, meant brothels.

SPEAKING MY MIND

Drifting in the world, lost in a drunken stupor,
recalling tiny waists and dancers on my palm.
Waking now from that ten-year Yangzhou dream,
what have I gained but the name of a heartless cad?

遣懷

落魄江湖載酒行，
楚腰纖細掌中輕。
十年一覺揚州夢，
贏得青樓薄倖名。

8

The Mysterious Mr. Li Shangyin 李商隱

We begin this chapter with a musical instrument, the *se* 瑟, predecessor to the *qin* 琴, and the *zheng* 箏, each translated, at times, as zithers or lutes in English. *Se* 瑟 is pronounced "sut" in Cantonese and "suh" in Mandarin. It does not exist anymore, or you might say it exists in the form of the *qin* and the *zheng*. It is said that the mythological King Fu Xi was the one who invented the *se*, which originally had fifty strings. Whether it was Fu Xi himself or Huang Di, the Yellow Emperor who came after him, who reduced the *se*'s number of strings from fifty to twenty-five depends on who is telling the story. Whichever emperor did this, the story is that when the White Maiden, a virtuosa of the *se*, was summoned to play on that fateful occasion, the music's sadness overwhelmed the emperor who ordered her to stop. When she refused to stop, he took the instrument from her and, in his rage, split it in half. That was how the *se* came to have only twenty-five strings instead of fifty.

Li Shangyin's celebrated poem called Jin Se 錦瑟, may be translated as "The Brocade or Adorned *Se*". No one is quite sure why he called it that, except to say it implies that this is a treasured, and therefore decorated, instrument. What it represents, its mystery, is open to interpretation.

The scholar in the second couplet is Zhuangzi 莊子 (Chuangtzu in Wade-Giles), who famously asked on waking from a dream "was it I who dreamed I was a butterfly or is it the butterfly dreaming it is me?" The king is King Wang, where 望 *wang* is the word for hope. He is a mythical King of Shu who accomplished great things for his people and then gave his throne to his counsellor, Bie Ling 鱉靈. He then disappeared into the woods and turned into a cuckoo. There are several versions giving different reasons for why that happened:

1. He thought Bie Ling would make a better king than himself, but power corrupted this good man, and King Wang had to come back from seclusion to awaken his conscience. When King Wang died, he turned into a cuckoo and every spring came out of the forest to remind his people they must work the fields to reap the riches of the land.

2. King Wang had a passionate affair with Bie Ling's wife when he sent Bie to tame the floods. Afterwards, he regretted the betrayal and gave his throne to Bie Ling, while he himself flew into the mountains and became a cuckoo. This cuckoo spat blood when he sang, and the blood turned into the azalea. Which is why both bird, cuckoo, and flower, azalea, are called 杜鵑 *dujuan* in Chinese. King Wang's birth name is Du Yu 杜宇, the same *du* as the flower and the bird.

3. A third version of the story has Bie Ling usurping the throne and driving King Wang into the woods, and that is why King Wang turned into a cuckoo, singing such a sad song that when people heard it they remembered his story. This cuckoo also spits blood and the blood turns into azaleas.

FRIENDS AND LOVERS

Now, Li Shangyin's line reads: "King Wang gave his heart in spring to the cuckoo for safekeeping." Since the heart inclines towards romance in the spring, the poet is probably alluding to the story of the affair.

The third couplet speaks of the phenomena of pearl-making and jade-smoking. One cannot be certain whether Li Shangyin was aware that pearls are born of an irritant trapped in the oyster. In any case, jade and pearl are both living things in the Chinese imagination. In the case of jade, the stone or jade can come alive after absorbing the energy of generations of suns and moons. Jade is also supposed to protect one from harm, even physical harm, which is why when you fall, for example, the piece of jade breaks instead of you! Families are known to have passed jade on from one generation to another and one is supposed to wear it against one's skin so that the stone can absorb one's warmth and energy and, over time, mythical time that is, the piece of stone is supposed to become more and more translucent.

THE MYSTERIOUS SE

> No one knows how these fifty-strings came about:
> each fret and string recall a glowing year of youth.
> Scholar Zhuang lost at dawn in a butterfly's dream.
> King Wang gave his heart to the cuckoo's charge.
> Vast seas, moon-brightened: oysters cry pearls.
> Blue fields, sun-warmed: jade breathes smoke.
> How can I keep this feeling within reach,
> I'm lost in confusion even as it emerges.

Second attempt:

MY CHINA IN TANG POETRY

THE DECORATED SE

No beginning, no reason, these fifty-strings.
Each fret, each string, describes a vital year.
Zhuangzi woke up and lost himself in a butterfly dream.
King Wang, aroused in spring, gave his heart to a cuckoo.
Under vast seas, beneath bright moons, pearls have tears.
Across blue fields, warmed by the sun, jade comes alive.
Can this great passion be retrieved from memory,
elusive as it is even at the moment of experience.

錦瑟

錦瑟無端五十弦，
一弦一柱思華年。
莊生曉夢迷蝴蝶，
望帝春心託杜鵑。
滄海月明珠有淚，
藍田日暖玉生煙。
此情可待成追憶，
只是當時已惘然。

GIFT OF THE LOTUS PLANT

Flowers and their leaves do not receive equal attention,
flowers are put in gold vases and leaves are left to rot.
Only the lotuses with their bright green leaves and pink-red buds,
furl and unfurl, open and close, leaves and flowers, in harmony.
These flowers and these leaves show each other off, till
one fades and the other withers, and that's a sad sight to see.

FRIENDS AND LOVERS

贈荷花

世間花葉不相倫，
花入金盆葉作塵。
惟有綠荷紅菡萏，
卷舒開合任天真。
此花此葉長相映，
翠減紅衰愁殺人。

Some say this poem was written for his wife, and seeing as the theme is that of a flower whose leaves and blossoms enhance each other, as in a good marriage, the conjecture makes sense. By all accounts, despite talk of secret lovers, Li Shangyin loved his wife and had a happy marriage. Nevertheless, marrying her was not an easy decision, because her father was considered siding with the "Li faction", whereas Li Shangyin's mentor was of the "Niu faction". As mentioned in the Preamble, the contentious Li and Niu factions plagued the Tang court at this time. Thus, the marriage put our poet in the awkward position of being viewed as ungrateful to his teacher by, as it were, marrying into the other side. Long story short, because of this, many obstacles impeded his progress towards recognition and success. The following poem was probably written after he experienced such hardship from rejection by members of the Niu faction which was gaining the upper hand at the time.

MY CHINA IN TANG POETRY

FALLEN FLOWERS

The guests have left. On the balcony I watch
flowers fly in chaotic flurries over the garden,
falling in disarray along the crooked pathway,
as the slanting rays lengthen into the distance.
Too sad, I have yet to sweep up the fallen reds,
still hoping they will return to spring's favor and
come back to greet my fond heart. But spring too
is ending, and all that's left is this tarnished robe.

落花

高閣客竟去，
小園花亂飛。
參差連曲陌，
迢遞送斜暉。
腸斷未忍掃，
眼穿仍欲歸。
芳心向春盡，
所得是沾衣。

FRIENDS AND LOVERS

SENT TO ONE IN THE NORTH

You asked me when I can come home, but I have yet no answer for you.
Autumn rain on Mount Ba is flooding the rocky ponds and rivers tonight.
I imagine the two of us sitting side by side at our window someday soon,
trimming a candle wick, reminiscing about the night it rained so hard on Mount Ba.

夜雨寄北

君問歸期未有期，
巴山夜雨漲秋池。
何當共剪西窗燭，
卻話巴山夜雨時。

People have said that the "one in the north" is either his wife, or a lover, or a friend. All can agree that this was written during the years when he was sent south to the Ba region in Sichuan when he was thirty-nine to forty-three years old. His wife, however, had died soon after he left "the north," so if it was addressed to her, he had not heard the news. In any case, most people have found this apparently simple, little poem very moving. And indeed, if he was writing to a ghost without knowing it, it would make the poem even more poignant.

Li Shangyin's 無題 "Untitled" poems are deservedly well-loved and quoted by lovers across the centuries, mostly disgruntled or frustrated lovers. There are fifteen, some say twenty of them. Here are eight. I am calling each of them a "Song Without a Name". Seven are written in seven-character regulated verse, Number 6 is a *jueju*. There have been many studies and speculations as to who he was writing about or to whom he was writing, and whether this mystery person was one particular person or several different ones. Because of the cloak-and-dagger nature of the poems, speculations mostly revolve around forbidden or illicit love affairs. The likely candidates seem to be three possibilities: One, a Daoist nun; two, his patron's wife or concubine; or, three, someone high-ranking, like a princess or a prince's mistress, at different times in his life. And, some could even be addressed to his wife, dead or alive.

EIGHT SONGS WITHOUT A NAME 八首無題詩
(in no particular order and need not be read together)

Note: Peng Lai, you remember, means paradise.

1

Hard to see you, hard to let you go:
East Wind falters, all flowers die.
Spring worms spin till their silk is spent.
When wax turns to ashes, tears will dry.
The morning mirror tells no lies,
night songs sharpen the moon's cold rays.
Peng Lai is not so far from here:
go, go my bluebirds, spy me out a way.

FRIENDS AND LOVERS

相見時難別亦難，
東風無力百花殘。
春蠶到死絲方盡，
蠟炬成灰淚始乾。
曉鏡但愁雲鬢改，
夜吟應覺月光寒。
蓬山此去無多路，
青鳥殷勤為探看。

In the next poem he talks about being impatient that the ink is not darkening. This is because he has to grind an ink stick on the inkwell to make ink before he can dip his brush in to start writing.

2

Coming is an empty word, and when you go you are untraceable.
The moon slants low into my loft, announces the fifth-night hour.
Even in dreams you are far away. Birds elicit no answering calls.
I'm writing you in a hurry, impatient at the ink for not darkening.
In the candlelight, green-gold kingfishers are caged in shadows,
embroidered waterlilies lie on my pillow, exude a musky scent.
Remember how that prince complained about the distance to Peng Lai?
For us, our paradise is even farther, beyond ten thousand hills away.

MY CHINA IN TANG POETRY

來是空言去絕蹤，
月斜樓上五更鐘。
夢爲遠別啼難喚，
書被催成墨未濃。
蠟照半籠金翡翠，
麝薰微度繡芙蓉。
劉郎已恨蓬山遠，
更隔蓬山一萬重。

In the next poem, 1) the moon-toad is the incense or incense burner, and the jade-tiger is a garden ornament; 2) Jia's daughter is in a story from the Western Jin (266-316), involving elopement and eventual marriage; and 3) Lady Fu is found in another Three Kingdoms story involving Cao Cao's two sons loving the same woman.

3

Sa-sa the east wind comes, spattering rain.
Above the pond of waterlilies, thunderclouds groan.
The moon-toad has sharp teeth, he's nibbled through the incense.
The jade-tiger has a long neck, he dangles in circles over the well.
Jia's daughter spied herself a husband through a slit in the screen.
All Lady Fu left the King of Wei is a cold pillow. Passion
cannot compete with the force of spring: buds will bloom.
One inch of longing, one inch of ashes.

FRIENDS AND LOVERS

颯颯東風細雨來，
芙蓉塘外有輕雷。
金蟾嚙鎖燒香入，
玉虎牽絲汲井回。
賈氏窺簾韓掾少，
宓妃留枕魏王才。
春心莫共花爭發，
一寸相思一寸灰。

4

Layer upon layer of silk bed curtains like a scented phoenix's tail,
stitch into stitch sewn together, emerald waves crowning its canopy,
you blush, remembering, trying to hide behind your moon-shaped fan,
as your carriage passes by, leaving me only with its thunderous noise.
This room was not empty once; together, we watched the candles dim.
Cut off now, not a word from you, pomegranates have turned red since.
And my dappled horse is tethered to the drooping willow by the river.
When will the southwest wind blow this way and bring warmth again?

鳳尾香羅薄幾重，
碧文圓頂夜深縫。
扇裁月魄羞難掩，
車走雷聲語未通。

MY CHINA IN TANG POETRY

曾是寂寥金燼暗，
斷無消息石榴紅。
斑騅只繫垂楊岸，
何處西南任好風。

The Tearless Maid in the next poem is a character in an old *yuefu*. In Chinese, her name is 莫愁, meaning, "No/Not/Don't/Won't [be] Sad/Miserable". 莫 also happens to be a not too uncommon last name, but who would name their daughter Misery even if their last name means "No"?

5

Thick curtains trap darkness in the room of the Tearless Maid;
she's been waiting for the autumn dawn as the hours lengthen.
A goddess lives, from the beginning, on the verge of a dream.
There's a young girl in an old book, never ever known a lover.
Wind fighting waves, beating down on tender caltrop leaves.
In moonlight and dewdrops, why do cassias smell so sweet?
I'll tell it to you straight: no good can come of this yearning.
Just let it go, let it break, and shatter this crystalline madness.

重幃深下莫愁堂，
臥後清宵細細長。
神女生涯原是夢，
小姑居處本無郎。
風波不信菱枝弱，
月露誰教桂葉香？
直道相思了無益，
未妨惆悵是清狂。

The last line of this next *jueju* brings Xishi into the picture for good measure, to describe the lady both as a goddess and as Xishi, King Wu's consort.

6.

I've heard people speak of a goddess called Green Blossom, and gazed to the ends of the horizon to catch a glimpse of her. Who'd have known, after all these years, I'd be given a chance to steal a glance at her in King Wu's secret garden last night.

聞道閶門萼綠華，
昔年相望抵天涯。
豈知一夜秦樓客，
偷看吳王苑內花。

The fourth line of the next poem reads in Chinese, 心有靈犀一點通, "our hearts are linked like the rhinoceros's horn," referring to the understanding between lovers. This expression comes from the belief that the rhinoceros' horn is extremely sensitive and able to pass information from its tip instantly to its brain. an expression still in common usage today, although I doubt if many know that the rhinoceros or its horn are involved. They are playing a party game so there are other people present; therefore they are exchanging glances between them (secret hooks). Finally, Orchid Terrace is the name of an administrative department building where the poet was an official.

7.

Last night's dawn star brought on last night's wind.
On the east side of Cassia Hall, west of the gallery:

had we wings we'd fly, a pair of rainbow phoenixes.
Our hearts are linked; we have no need for words.
Playing a guessing game, exchanging secret hooks,
under the red flare of candlelight, spring wine warm:
too soon, drums summoned me to Orchid Terrace
and I galloped away like tumbleweed in the wind.

昨夜星辰昨夜風，
畫樓西畔桂堂東。
身無彩鳳雙飛翼，
心有靈犀一點通。
隔座送鉤春酒暖，
分曹射覆蠟燈紅。
嗟余聽鼓應官去，
走馬蘭台類轉蓬。

Poem 8 begins in music; the *zheng* is a stringed instrument I discussed at the beginning of this chapter. We meet a Princess Li Yang here. She is the favorite daughter of the King of Southern Liang (507-557). She was forced to marry Hou Jing in 549 when she was fourteen. Hou Jing was an unscrupulous and ambitious general who, long story short, ended up killing both her grandfather and her father and made himself king. The people so hated him that when they finally killed him, his body was preserved and roasted and eaten by those who could get their hands on the meat; even his bones were consumed. His wife, the former Princess Li Yang, was forced to eat a piece of him as well in order to avenge her father, her grandfather, and her country. The only reason I can give for her story being placed here is that it is in contrast to the unmarried "old" maiden in the village. Is Li Shangyin asking which of them has the better fate? Also, I am unable to say for certain why Qing Ming is brought into the picture here, unless it is referring to an actual event that happened after this rainy spring festival. Was our poet hiding behind the wall with his lover? What were they watching or keeping watch for? All we know is that whatever they did, it kept him up that night.

8.

> Where is that sad zheng chasing the fast flute music coming from?
> Cherries blooming down every lane all the way to the willow banks.
> In the house on the east is a maiden past her prime, still unmarried;
> the day is growing late, and the third month of the year is half over.
> Princess Li Yang was fourteen when she was given away to a brute.
> It was on a warm Qing Ming day when we peeked behind the wall.
> That night, I tossed and turned and tossed till the fifth night hour.
> The swallows in my rafters must have heard my long, long sighs.

何處哀箏隨急管，
櫻花永巷垂楊岸。
東家老女嫁不售，
白日當天三月半。
溧陽公主年十四，
清明暖後同牆看。
歸來展轉到五更，
梁間燕子聞長嘆。

MY CHINA IN TANG POETRY

Li Shangyin also wrote many poems about willows, and apparently there was a woman named Willow early on in his life.

WILLOWS

Once upon a time you joined the east wind at Spring Garden
and danced for us, when all things were heartbreakingly new.
How is it you have lasted into this chilly fall season today,
bringing in the slanting sun and the crickets' mournful cry?

柳

曾逐東風拂舞筵，
樂遊春苑斷腸天。
如何肯到清秋日，
已帶斜陽又帶蟬 。

"Kingdom's Fall", you remember, is a cliché for a beautiful woman, so beautiful she brings down a kingdom, like the face that launched a thousand ships. We have met quite a few by now, and their beauty is often attributed to their lovely eyebrows. Willows, too, are often used to describe beautiful women, usually linked to movement, for obvious reasons.

WILLOW

Spring moves in and innumerable leaves come with it.
Dawn peers through countless branches into the day.
Can willows understand what it is to long for another,
dancing, dancing like that with no thought of resting?
Catkins fly everywhere, confusing butterflies among them,
branches sensually swaying, exposing orioles behind them.

FRIENDS AND LOVERS

Kingdom's Fall, every single one of them,
their beauty is far more than that of pretty brows.

柳

動春何限葉，
撼曉幾多枝。
解有相思否，
應無不舞時。
絮飛藏皓蝶，
帶弱露黃鸝。
傾國宜通體，
誰來獨賞眉。

In the next poem, the "Seven Sages of the Bamboo Grove" make another appearance mostly because they are associated with bamboo. Bamboo, pines, and willows are all decorative trees. Here, the reference is to King Qi of the Southern Dynasty who built a shrine and planted "thousands" of rows of willows around it.

WEEPING WILLOWS

Willows like young girls dancing in the Imperial Garden,
lifting and sweeping all along the Crooked Lake,
their jade ornaments tinkling, dangling along after them,
their heavenly costumes flying with the gentle breeze.
Jin's Seven Virtuous Men took over the bamboo grove,
current luminaries are epitomized by the illustrious pine.
Now that you have been chosen for ancestral palaces,
who is there left to brighten up common empty shrines?

MY CHINA IN TANG POETRY

垂柳

娉婷小苑中，
婀娜曲池東。
朝佩皆垂地，
仙衣盡帶風。
七賢寧佔竹，
三品且饒松。
腸斷靈和殿，
先皇玉座空。

Zhang Tai Road in the next poem is at the capital.

WILLOW
(Written in Ba at Shu, longing to be back at the capital.)

Willow reflection in the water stirs my sleeping passions. Look closer and you'll see my homesick heart pounding like thunder rumbling in the faraway hills of Ba in Shu, like horses' hooves clopping along Zhang Tai Road.

柳

柳映江潭底有情，
望中頻遣客心驚。
巴雷隱隱千山外，
更作章臺走馬聲。

FRIENDS AND LOVERS

The Story of Chang'e 嫦娥

Chang'e is pronounced Charng + Uh (as in the *uh* part of "huh?") in Mandarin. Sorry. It doesn't sound very pretty in English. The characters are nevertheless beautiful: both have the woman radical, one is the word for "always" 常 and the other, for "I" 我.

Her story takes us back to the Queen Mother of the West, who gave Hou Yi a pill of everlasting life. Hou Yi is a mythological archer who saved the earth by shooting down nine out of ten suns which were scorching the earth. He left the one we now have so that the earth has enough light and warmth to keep life going. As a reward, the Queen Mother of the West gave him an elixir in the form of a pill. His wife was Chang'e. (Some say she was a maid in heaven for the Jade Emperor before descending to earth. Some just describe her as a very beautiful but otherwise ordinary mortal.) Anyway, the pill of immortality apparently was not consumed right away by Hou Yi. (Some say he was planning to share it with her, and some say since there was only one, he was saving it for himself, and perhaps he didn't want to leave her till he was ready to fly to heaven.) When he was out hunting one day, Chang'e swallowed the pill. (Some say out of curiosity; some, that she stole it; some that somebody else heard about the pill and tried to steal it, so she took it before he could get to it.) In any case, Hou Yi arrived home to see her sailing off into the sky. He tried to shoot her down. Some say he was so sad to see her go that he made moon cakes every year on the day she left, which was on the full moon of the eighth month of the lunar year. When Chang'e arrived on the moon, she was turned into a toad, the reason being that since the toad hibernates and comes back to life, as it were, in the spring, people used to think that it had undergone a rebirth, and since Chang'e had achieved immortality by swallowing the elixir, it was as if she had been resurrected. Thus, when she reached the moon, she simply became what she was originally. (That is why you see toads so often in jade carvings, especially in feng sui related items). As for the bunny we also see in the Chinese moon, some say it was sent to help her pound elixir pills, and some say it had always been there, pounding away.

CHANG'E

Candlelight on the mica screen makes blurry shadows glow.
The Silver River is slowly fading as the Morning Star sinks.
Chang'e must be regretting her theft of life everlasting by now,
night after night, alone, in the dark heart of the deep blue sea.

嫦娥

雲母屏風燭影深，
長河漸落曉星沉。
嫦娥應悔偷靈藥，
碧海青天夜夜心。

ON THE EVE OF THE MID-AUTUMN MOON

Under the low grass crickets hide, chattering about frost on
　the leaves.
In the distance, a jewelled tower shines on the smooth water
　of the lake.
Rabbit and toad huddle in the cold among the white cassias
　in the moon.
She must be sad tonight, Chang'e, trapped in memory on a
　night like this.

FRIENDS AND LOVERS

月夕

草下陰蟲葉上霜，
朱欄迢遞壓湖光。
兔寒蟾冷桂花白，
此夜姮娥應斷腸。

In the last of the three poems, Chang'e has a rival on the moon. She is the Frost Goddess, whose duty is to start the frost in late autumn. The sound of crickets announces the beginning of fall, the flight of wild geese south announces mid-autumn, and the first frost tells us it is late autumn. I have translated Li Shangyin's name for Chang'e here, which is 素娥 or "White/Blanch Beauty," as "White Moth" because it seems to me "White Moth" works better with "Frost Goddess." But why moth? Because the second character in Chang'e's name is homophonous with the word for moth: one is written with a woman radical and the other a worm radical. Also, the second character, "e," means beautiful woman, and beautiful women are described as having moth brows (referring to the antennae.) I have conflated the two. If you cannot accept my explanation, feel free to substitute Chang'e for "White Moth" in the translation.

MY CHINA IN TANG POETRY

A FROSTY MOON

First calls of wild geese going south break the silence left by cicadas.
In the distance, a tall tower is standing where the water meets the sky.
They can both endure the cold, Frost Goddess and White Moth, but
who, between them, can claim the title of the fairest lady in the moon?

霜月

初聞征雁已無蟬,
百尺樓高水接天。
青女素娥俱耐冷,
月中霜里鬥嬋娟。

In youth, I had preferred the mysterious and beautiful "Song[s] Without a Name" among Li Shangyin's poems. Now, I find this next *jueju* just as moving, if not more. My mother, I remember, often quoted the last two lines.

FRIENDS AND LOVERS

PLEASURE GARDEN ON THE ANCIENT PLAIN

Restless and in a mood, I went out riding
up to this garden with its celebrated view.
The sunset wraps me in a lavish embrace
only to say that night is fast approaching.

登樂遊原
向晚意不適，
驅車登古原。
夕陽無限好，
只是近黃昏。

Endnote: Verse Forms

The oldest book of Chinese poetry is the *Shijing*, 詩經, often translated as the *Book of Songs*, mainly folk songs collected from as early as the first millennium BCE. Confucius (551 BCE-479 BCE) is said to have been its final editor. Poetry is generally referred to as *shi*, and *jing* means collection. The vocabulary and culture of the *Shijing* is associated with the northern region of China. The dominant line of a poem in the *Shijing* is four characters.

In the south comes another important collection of early poetry called the *Chu Ci* 楚辭 (dated back to The Warring States, ca. 475-221 BCE). The *Chu Ci* is made up of several books, the most important of which is the *Li Sao* 離騷, a lament attributed to Qu Yuan 屈原 (340 BCE-278 BCE). The poems in the *Chu Ci* vary in line lengths and their imagery is associated with the State of Chu 楚. Much flora and fauna are found in poetry both north and south.

During the Han Dynasty 漢 (206 BCE-227 CE) the classic *shi* 詩 with its four-character lines was revived, and a new development of poems of five- and seven-character lines emerged. In addition, there had been a Music Bureau, or department of music in court found as early as the mythical government of Huang Di, 黃帝, who has been credited with starting a whole slew of things, including astronomy, math, writing characters, sericulture, musical laws and a Chinese version of football, the taming of wild beasts, the string instrument, guqin, and even invention of upper and lower garments and the weaving and dyeing of cloth. There is little documentary evidence though that the Music Bureau existed until the Qin 秦 (221-205 BCE) and into the Han dynasties.

FRIENDS AND LOVERS

Some Verse Forms Popularly Used In the Tang Dynasty (618–907)

The Tang Dynasty is often referred to as the Golden Age of Poetry in China. Poets of this period freely adopted and refined past verse forms and new forms were crystallized. The *lushi*, 律詩, was perfected early in the dynasty. It is a five- or seven-character, eight-line composition with prescribed tonal and rhyme schemes, calling for parallel structure in the middle, that is, second and third couplets. It is often translated as "regulated verse" in English. Then came the *jueju* 绝句, which was an outgrowth of the *lushi*. This is a four-line, five- or seven-character poem. That means it is half a *lushi*, and thus, is often translated as "curtailed" or "truncated" verse. The tonal patterns of the *lushi* are kept but the parallel structure is made optional, although the couplet remains foundational to the form. We think of it as a *lushi* cut short. The aesthetics of the *jueju* are similar to the Japanese haiku (which was inspired by the *jueju*) in that it invites one to contemplate and further ruminate on its meaning as it ends and is judged by its economy and suggestiveness. The *pailu* 排律 also started to emerge. This is a long form of the *lushi*, and length is not prescribed, so long as it runs in couplets. These are all called New Style Verse 近體詩 in the Tang dynasty.

Then, there is the *gushi*, 古詩, with *gu* meaning "old-style" or "ancient" and *shi* meaning "verse." It was the *yuefu* 樂府 that led the way to its development with the broader use of rhyme and fewer metrical restrictions. In the Tang dynasty, its use was revived and is differentiated from regulated verse by not following, or even deliberately violating, the rules of the *lushi*.

The *yuefu* itself was a form of poetry derived from folk-ballads. Yue fu means "music/bureau," and the poetic form is named after the governmental department of music by that name. (The character "*fu*" here is not to be confused with another word, "*fu*,"

MY CHINA IN TANG POETRY

赋 of the same sound but not the same tone, and a different word altogether, meaning "ode" or "rhapsody.") The Music Bureau in the Han dynasty collected folksongs. Confucius said that folk songs represented the voice of the people. The musical scores from these songs were used for ceremonial occasions at court as well. This collection of folk poetry from the Han dynasty serves as the basis of the *yuefu* form. These poems consisted of lines of varying lengths and broke away from the older four-character line by their use of the five-character. Tang poets imitated these *yuefu* ballads and made up their own poems accordingly. Du Fu and Bai Juyi were both promoters of this form.

Poets and Dates

In Volume I: *Superstars*
Li Bai or Li Bo (Li Po)	701 – 762
Du Fu (Tu Fu)	712 – 770

In Volume II: *Floating on Clouds*
Meng Haoran (Meng Hao-jan)	689/91 – 740
Wang Wei (Wang Wei)	699 – 761
Li Ye (Li Ye)	737? – 784
Xue Tao (Hsueh T'ao)	768 – 831
Liu Caichun (Liu Ts'ai – ts'un)	uncertain
Yu Xuanji (Yu Hs'uan-chi)	844 – 871

In Volume III: *Friends and Lovers*
Liu Zongyuan (Liu Chungyuan)	773 – 819
Liu Yuxi (Liu Yushi)	772 – 842
Bai Juyi (Po Chu-i)	772 – 846
Yuan Zhen (Yuan Chen)	779 – 831
Li He (Li Ho)	790 – 816
Du Mu (Tu Mu)	803 – 852
Li Shangyin (Li Shang-yin)	812 – 858

Acknowledgements

Many of these poems have been with me since childhood, but it was in telling my mother's story after her passing that I felt the urgency of putting together these translations for others. At the same time, my friend, Virginia Raymond, suggested that we start a writing group. Nancy Vine Durling immediately responded, and since then, the three of us, with occasional visitors, have been meeting sporadically for reading and writing sessions. Virginia, an attorney and Latin American literature professor, Nancy, a medieval French scholar and translator, and I come from entirely different backgrounds, bringing fresh perspectives to each other's work, both sympathetic and critical. This variety of input reminds me of the poetry and translation workshops at Princeton where, as an undergraduate, I began to develop an eye and an ear for writing beyond myself. I must especially acknowledge my teachers, John Peck, Edmund Keeley, and Charles Tomlinson, who took my writing seriously, more so than I could have done myself, and gave me the confidence and critical training that never left me. I must also thank all the students who participated in the translation workshops I attended throughout my years at Princeton, all coming with different languages and cultures, who shared their work with me as I with them, as we pounced on each other with youthful criticism and appreciation. Among these cohorts, Nadia Benabid has remained a staunch comrade in verse long after we both left graduate school. A big thank you is due also to the Fates who led me to Earnshaw Books and the "yes" from Mr. Graham Earnshaw, whose keen eye saw the merits of this series of Tang poems and helped me launch them into the world. And, I am in debt to to my friends, Jim Earl and Laura Gibbs, who have read many of these pages and hunted down my stray commas and miscellaneous mistakes.

To my mother, who sowed the seeds of love of classical Chinese poetry in me, and to David, my life-support and partner, I have no words that can fully express my gratitude. To Su Zhong, the first person I turn to whenever I have Chinese questions, and my high school and kindergarten classmates from Hong Kong scattered all over the world who have remained close and encouraging; to Mrs. O'Connell, the fiery speech teacher at Diocesan Girls' School who first taught me how to breathe and dance to the rhythms of English poetry, how can I thank you for the gifts you have given me?

In addition, there have been sympathetic listeners that kept me afloat, both friends and strangers, some of whom are no longer with us. I am grateful to them all. At a few junctures of my writing life when I might have given up, encouragement came my way from such writers and critics as James J.Y. Liu, who was Yvonne Sung-Sheng Chang's mentor and who led her to me for the translation of Wang Wen-Hsing's important Modernist novel, *Jia Bian (Family Catastrophe)*, and Wang Wen-Hsing himself; Stephen Soong, who held up an issue of *Renditions* from going to press in order to wait for my small contribution, and who was generous enough to say that he heard the Chinese poems in my English, which, apparently, was a new experience for him; and Joseph S.M. Lau, who, sadly, passed away recently, and who also showed an interest in my translations and gave me the chance to work on some stories he collected in the *Columbia Anthology of Modern Chinese Literature*. I am grateful also to have met all my students through the years, from the one who said I was the only professor who kept him awake in class, to Robert Emerson who told me my poetry "kicks ass," and Beatrice Halbach-Singh who has become a close friend and enthusiastic listener, and all my readers wherever you are, and particularly the anonymous reader, "James," who reviewed *A River in Springtime* on "Goodreads" and called it "masterful."

Finally, to my daughter, Anne 天菲, who is the guru in my life, and my son, Zachary 甘苇, prominent in my mind as representing future generations in the Chinese Diaspora as well as poetry lovers everywhere, this is for you.

Epilogue

Growing up in Hong Kong, I did not do well in Chinese classes, and often received "big eggs", meaning zeroes, for Chinese "dictation" In this context, dictation means writing out assigned texts for memorization at home, and then writing them out in class, usually from classical Chinese poetry. In addition, such "dictations" had to be done with Chinese ink brushes, not an easy task for little hands to accomplish. Being neither studious nor particularly good at rote learning, I have no fond memories of such endeavors. On the other hand, I was fortunate to have a mother who loved the Chinese classics and would "sing" or "chant" poems and tell stories from them to me, and I absorbed by osmosis. It was not until I left the British colony for college that I discovered Chinese classical poetry for myself. Or you might say, when what I absorbed was given space to bloom.

My favorite poems were from the Tang and Song periods, and my love was discovered through English translation exercises. These exercises began at the Creative Writing workshops ran by the poet John Peck when I was an undergraduate at Princeton, and I continued taking these workshops as a graduate student under such poets as Edmund Keeley and Charles Tomlinson. I shall forever be grateful to them for what they sparked and helped nurture in me. In these workshops, I learned to borrow voices, making English poetry through listening to ghosts, the ancient Chinese poets whom my mother had sung to me all those years ago. Eventually, translation became an integral part of my work as a writer.

Translations follow originals. The music, images, and ideas

MY CHINA IN TANG POETRY

in the Chinese poems I translated were not of my own creation, did not come out of my own experience. Still, the more I wrote and translated the more I came to realize the understanding translation demands is not so different from the discoveries that grew out of my own writings. In other words, all writing is translation, from thoughts to words, and all translations, especially of poetry, are works of creative writing even though reading and understanding some other person's work and his or her culture precede the translator's creation. Translation is both greedy and generous, it wishes to appropriate as it wants to share and disseminate.

Let me now turn the coin onto its other side. The expression "lost in translation" acknowledges that not everything in one culture or language can be brought into another language or culture. Translation is, if not impossible, quixotic. I do not, however, agree with those who think that what comes across in translation only reveals that which cannot be translated, which is, after all what the phrase, "lost in translation" usually implies, that is, the failure of translation. Clearly, more is demanded of the reader of translations, just as more is demanded of the citizen of one culture to engage with those of other cultures. One must first be willing to take the leap of imagination into another world, and often, another period of time, in order to be a successful reader of translations. On the other hand, the more different the culture, the more one may be looking for differences, surprises, strangeness even. Perhaps that is why so many translations of Chinese classical poems especially have been allowed, even encouraged, to sound strange, foreign, and sometimes, weird, even nonsensical. Let me assure you that although there are Chinese poets who endeavor to "make it new" and surprise readers in their own culture with experimentation and refreshing choices, Chinese poetry is no more awkward or nonsensical than

English poetry. In other words, I am asking you to recognize poor expressions and bad poetry for what they are, and not expect or excuse them just because they are found in translations. To do so is to disrespect the art of translation, to denigrate the challenge it poses.

Since our world has simultaneously expanded and shrunk, I shall not belabor the point about the importance of cultural exchange and exposure. The shortcut to the heart of Chinese culture is through its classics. As the popular Chinese saying goes, "to the people, food is heaven." Let me add that classical poetry is second in importance to the Chinese people only to its cuisine. Chinese people everywhere quote from classical Chinese poetry, both to express themselves and to impress others. Lines from the Tang poet Li Bai's poem, "The Road to Shu is Hard," showed up in a popular rap performance in China not so long ago. There is even a rock band named Tang Dynasty in China. Classical Chinese poetry, especially Tang poetry, is very much a part of contemporary Chinese life. Beyond prosperity and power, the Tang dynasty is judged as significant also because of its receptive and adventurous characteristics. It is, as Mark Edward Lewis calls it, *China's Cosmopolitan Empire*, (The Belknap Press of Harvard University Press, 2012).

Few will disagree that the two giants or superstars of Tang poetry are Li Bai and Du Fu (also known as Li Po and Tu Fu in previous translations). There are many translations of their works into other languages, especially into English. Why, then, do I find it necessary to translate these poets again? My first answer is that translation is a performance art, and as with any great piece of music, each performance, especially the better ones, will have its own contributions to make. The second reason is that although there are many prose translations of these poems, and some in verse as well, many of these poems

MY CHINA IN TANG POETRY

are still waiting to be "rescued," to use David Young's reasoning in his *Du Fu: A Life in Poetry* (Knopf, 2008). When the Modernist poet Ezra Pound spoke of "making it [poetry] new", he meant that translating another culture's poetry can be used to refresh or transform one's own culture and poetry. Some poets have even "made [their own] poetry new" with no knowledge of the language from which they were translating. Pound himself, working from a crib, without knowing Chinese at the time, had done a better job than sinologists or Chinese translators with "The River Merchant's Wife", a poem by Li Bai, whom he called by his Japanese name, Rihaku. To give any translation a fair hearing, we must remember that translation is not a secondary art but a performance art.

Music, image, meaning, context, and culture are all important to poetry, and of all these elements, music is the hardest to convey. The task I set for myself is to do the best I can with the music I hear in the original Chinese poems, which I hear in Cantonese, and bring it over into my English translations as poetry. At the turn of the last century, the Chinese translations into English, whether in Britain or in America, tended to be too sing-songy or tried too hard to force a rhyme. After Pound and the Imagists and their efforts to "make it new", English translations from the Chinese have tended towards directness or experimentation. The better poets who translate today have managed to avoid fussiness, archaic expressions, passive descriptions and the not-so-subtle rhymes and rhythms in their work. The voice of the poet-translator, however, often takes precedence over the original poet's voice, so that poems from different Chinese poets sound alike in translations done by the same English or American poet. In such cases, the poems that result should more accurately be called "appropriations" or "conversations" rather than translations. An appropriation is the result of the poet taking a Chinese poem, mixing it with his or her own experience of a similar sentiment, tailoring it to suit her or his own feel of it, and cutting or building a new poem out of it. That seems to be acceptable these days, and some interesting pieces have come from the practice, but I cannot agree with calling this exercise translation or a faithful rendition of the original.

With that, I go back to my starting point. Translations follow originals. The creativity in this act is different though no less demanding than original compositions. Translators are obliged to be true to the original even as they make the most of their own resources. To appropriate without being faithful is to circumvent the demands of the art of translation. As I see it, my role as translator is not to give my voice to the original poet, but to borrow as I lend, that is, to reproduce in English with my ventriloquist's skill the voice I hear in the Chinese, and to place again the poem where I found it, in its historical and cultural contexts as best I can. It is my duty, in translating, to attempt to differentiate each individual poet's style one from the other. I am helped in this last challenge by the Chinese poet's own choice of form and content, as well as by his or her own personality and the stories they tell. Those interested in prosody should consult my chapter on "Verse Forms" at the end of each volume.

My China in Tang Poetry is the culmination of all the above discoveries, driven not only by my own love of the stories and poems but also by my desire to make what I know and love accessible to others who have no Chinese, at least, no classical Chinese and therefore have no way into that world. This series is my offer to take you with me to visit my ghosts.

About The Author

Susan Wan Dolling is a Chinese American writer who was born in Hong Kong, attended the Diocesan Girls' School, studied in Japan, and graduated from Princeton University with an AB in English and Creative Writing PhD in Comparative Literature. She has taught English and Literature at Fordham University and Chinese Literature at the University of Texas at Austin. Her translations of modern Chinese literature and classical Chinese poetry can be found in such publications as *Another Chicago Magazine*, *Poetry Magazine*, *Words Without Border*, *Two Lines*, *The Columbia Anthology of Modern Chinese Literature*, and *Renditions*. Her translation of Wang Wen-Hsing's Modernist novel, *Family Catastrophe* is in University of Hawaii Press's Fiction from Modern China Series. *Superstars, Floating on Clouds* and *Friends and Lovers*, the three volumes of stories, readings, and translations in the series, *My China in Tang Poetry*, was published in 2024 by Earnshaw Books. Most recently, she and her cello teacher, Dr. Chi-Hui Kao, has formed a musical duo called "Note After Note." For more on Susan and her work, please visit www.susanwandolling.com.

www.ingramcontent.com/pod-product-compliance
Lightning Source LLC
LaVergne TN
LVHW010320070526
838199LV00065B/5618